Golden Oldies

Classic Bike Road Tests

Edited by Mike Nicks
Editor of Classic Bike

Tests by: Mike Nicks, Peter Watson, Royce Creasey, Val Ward, Jerry Clayton and Ted Davis.

PSL Patrick Stephens, Cambridge

Golden Oldies is published by Patrick Stephens Ltd, Bar Hill, Cambridge, CB3 8EL, in conjunction with EMAP National Publications Ltd, Peterborough.
Printed in England by Pindar Print Limited, Scarborough, North Yorkshire.

First published in 1981

ISBN 0 – 85059 – 571 – 1

Contents

4— 9	Introduction
10— 17	Aermacchi Ala Verde
18— 25	AJS Model 30
26— 33	Ambassador 250
34— 43	Ariel Arrow
44— 51	Ariel Red Hunter
52— 59	Ariel Square Four
60— 67	BSA Gold Star
68— 77	BSA Unit Twins
78— 85	Douglas 80 Plus
86— 93	Matchless G12
94— 99	Norton Dominator
100—105	OK Supreme
106—113	Royal Enfield Continental
114—121	Royal Enfield Interceptor
122—127	Rudge Ulster
128—135	Sunbeam S7 and S8
136—143	Triumph Thunderbird
144—151	Velocette MSS
152—160	Vincent Rapide and Comet

Introduction

Why does a certain perverse breed of motorcyclist prefer to ride obsolete motorcycles? If he or she bought new, there would be the opportunity to sample the huge performance of today's sports machines, and the undoubted reliability found in roadburners and commuter bikes alike. There is the chance to revel in the security of comprehensive guarantees that extend in some cases for two years, and the knowledge that a specialist dealer is never far away in the event of trouble.

Yet still this obstinate faction refuses to take advantage of the conveniences of life in the late twentieth century. For the same reasons that lead climbers to physically scale mountains instead of hiring helicopters to whisk them clinically to the peak, lovers of old bikes choose the arduous way of enjoying motorcycles. They mend their own, and in many cases even build their own machines.

This apparent eccentricity is in fact based on a number of extremely practical motives. In the first place parts for obsolete motorcycles, and particularly post-war British machines, are not necessarily hard to find. For all the more popular marques there exist dedicated dealers holding quite large stocks of components. Several owners' clubs run excellent spares manufacturing schemes, and second-hand parts can be found at autojumbles or via the small-ads columns of motorcycle magazines and weekly newspapers. At times it seems that bits for British bikes long out of production are even easier to come by than parts for brand new Japanese machines!

Another consideration in favour of the obsolete bike is cost. Often the crucial pieces needed to get a restored machine back on the road can be acquired relatively inexpensively. Some owners prefer to spend many hundreds of pounds in applying a showroom finish to a rebuilt bike. But it is also true that the less exotic machines, particularly the British vertical twins and pushrod singles of the post-war period, can be made into serviceable, hard-working bikes for perhaps £200 or £300.

In restoration costs, so much depends on an owner's mechanical abilities and range of equipment, but certainly an outlay of £500 can produce a machine that will prompt service station attendants to start the 'How old, how much, how fast' routine. Such a sum can hardly be termed extravagant these days.

Older bikes also have a less forbidding air about them should an owner have to delve into their internals. In ten years' time how many riders of the more complex Japanese bikes will wish to tear down a sixteen-valve twin-overhead-cam engine, or attempt a rescue project on the complex transmission system of an Oriental shaft-drive machine?

Even for skilled engineers willing to take on the challenge, the cost of parts will by then be massive — assuming, that is, that the necessary spares will be available. And as contemporary motorcycles become still more sophisticated (untouchable?) these problems will increase. Electronic black boxes, fuel injection, 120,000rpm turbochargers — these are not appropriate subjects for a homely spot of renovation in the garden shed on a summer's evening.

But enough of this talk of inexpensive costs and easy accessibility. Motorcyclists, whether they ride new bikes or old ones, are not thin-souled skinflints; the act of motorcycling itself, blurring down a country lane with the grey tarmac streaming beneath the wheels, is a highly emotional matter. The maintenance chores, the long restoration projects, are means to this end — the enjoyment of the motorcycle on a good road in the fresh air. This brings us back to our original question — why do some riders prefer relatively slow obsolete machines, when they could experience the thrill of today's 100bhp, 140mph projectiles? Few motorcycles that can now be termed

by Mike Nicks

Above: Quiet and respectable, the Sunbeam S7 had a long unhurried production run.

Below: This was the first lorry load of Triumphs to leave Meriden after the workers' blockade.

Above: The legendary Edward Turner on a post-war 'bathtub' 500cc Speed Twin somewhere in Wales.

Below: Gone but not forgotten, the James factory produced some great bikes, like this ISDT machine.

classics gave more than 50bhp, and most would not have exceeded the ton.

Again, there is really no mystery. For a start, it must be appreciated that the average rider is simply not capable of using to the full the performance potential of many modern bikes of 750cc and upwards. The fastest of these machines produce power outputs that Bob McIntyre, in 1957 the first man to lap the TT course at 100mph, could only have dreamed about. The road-riding motorcyclist will not be able to get around a 90mph corner at ten-tenths while accelerating a 100 horsepower — or even 80 horsepower — machine. So why buy what you cannot use?

But that is another of those mundane practical arguments. To return to the emotive side of the motorcycling experience itself, there is no doubt that many riders lament the absence of 'character' in modern machines. Exactly what constitutes character in a motorcycle is impossible to define, but one element most definitely involved is noise.

Ironically, the two Sunbeams tested in this book earned praise at the time of their manufacture for their quietness. But most motorcyclists like to hear an engine working, and in the innocent years before environmental considerations began to impinge on manufacturers, a motorcycle buyer usually got his share of satisfying noises. The Velocette MSS also tested here emits a leisurely beat so dependable you wish the pace of the world itself could be geared to it! An entirely different style of noise, an aggressive blare that will reign eternally as one of motorcycling's finest sounds, comes from vertical twins like the Triumph Thunderbird and Royal Enfield Interceptor. And for sheer deafening anti-social thunder, there is the marvellous crackle of the BSA Gold Star. Ah, reckless days . . .

Below: Always expensive, the HRD (and later Vincent) is amongst the elite of classic bikes.

Some modern bikes still sound marvellous. The deep pounding of a Ducati V-twin, the broken throb of a Laverda triple, the battle cry of a Japanese four approaching a five-figure rev counter reading, are the hallmarks of motorcycling in the 1980s. But the majority of machines, particularly the smaller ones, have had their lungs stifled. This is not entirely the manufacturers' fault — noise and emissions regulations are largely to blame.

Handling is another area in which some — by no means all — bikes from former eras excel over later arrivals. Earlier designers operated in a less oppressive atmosphere, not having to provide for luxury fittings such as electrical starters and indicators. Frames and cycle parts could also be lighter, as the engines produced relatively low outputs. In the best instances this produced machines with truly exceptional handling, like the 250cc Aermacchi Ala Verde tested in this volume. The Ala Verde makes some of today's 250cc machines appear flabby in appearance, soggy in corners, and not much faster in a straight line.

And even bikes not remembered for fabulous roadholding were at least compact. The 1,000cc Ariel Square Four weighed about 460lb dry; a square four designed today would probably scale 100lb more. The 1947 Vincent Rapide, an outstanding machine of its day with a top speed of 110mph, weighed about 470lb; the Yamaha TR1, a similar 1,000cc V-twin launched 34 years later, weighs nearly 500lb, produces 25bhp more, but is only some 10mph faster.

A straight comparison between the two is not possible, of course; the Vincent's designers had to cope with low-quality 'pool' petrol, Yamaha's engineers have to wrestle with power-sapping American noise and emissions regulations. But clearly, the creature comforts of modern machines have been obtained at the expense of agility.

But older motorcycles have an overall appeal that transcends individual qualities such as a fine exhaust note and compact handling. And this intriguing sensation is surely nothing more than the feeling the rider gets that he or she is operating something distinctly mechanical. Mechanical devices require sympathy, coaxing and maintenance — yet these are the very demands that many modern makers are trying to obliterate from their products.

The finest type of motorcyclist shuns the pre-packaged, total-convenience lifestyle (if he didn't he would long ago have abandoned his bike for a car). He's actually *interested* in what is happening inside his engine cases, and doesn't object to tending the machinery, assisting it to achieve optimum performance and reasonable longevity. Older motorcycles demand more of this treatment (although hypochondriac bikes that hardly ever see the road are to be avoided), and hence foster a two-way relationship between themselves and their owners. It's harder to feel so much for an antiseptic modern machine that merely demands a session with an electronic diagnostic tuning machine every 5,000 miles.

Let's clear one great misconception about old-bike fanatics. The intelligent ones are not bigots; they accept that contemporary motorcycles go faster for further than machines built in the post-vintage and post-war periods, and many enjoy owning 'moderns'. But they also say. "We like playing with the machinery of motorcycles as well as riding them, and therefore we'll also keep running our older bikes."

What exactly constitutes a test of a classic motorcycle? One type of assessment it does not consist of is a full-bore thrashing over thousands of miles, with a vicious session of speed testing through timing lights tossed in. The reason is obvious: the portals of Messrs Ariel, Vincent, Rudge, Royal Enfield, Douglas and Co have long since closed. Therefore a blown-up machine can hardly be tossed casually off the back of a trailer at the maker's service department with a request that it be ready for a resumption of testing in 48 hours. The bikes tested in this book were loaned by the generosity of private individuals, and in consequence were ridden sympathetically. Mechanical disasters or, even less forgiveable, crashes, would have ruined the results of a rebuild that may have taken many months.

This is not to say that test machines in the hands of *Classic Bike* are cosseted. They are ridden briskly enough for flaws to become apparent, but with empathy too. They are also ridden on appropriate roads. There would be no point in thrashing a Model 7 Norton Dominator for miles along a motorway; when our test machine was made in 1953 such highways were still years away. Instead, classic motorcycles are tested on classic roads – the beautiful, mature, 'A' and 'B' routes, coiling over hills and along valley floors, with which most of Britain still abounds. Perfect motorcycling territory, these roads — so why not use them to appreciate excellent machinery.

A further deviation from the format used in many magazines testing new motorcycles and cars is that the assessments have not been written to a set formula. The policy of *Classic Bike* has been instead to seek out writers with a special insight into the type of machinery involved, and to give them free rein in analysing the bikes. Thus none of these tests forms a litany of mere dry fact; comment and incisive interpretation is there in abundance.

Road tests that appeared in the British motorcycling periodicals in the forties, fifties and, to a lesser extent, the sixties had two grave flaws. Firstly, they were hopelessly uncritical of the machinery under scrutiny. And secondly, they were peppered with hideously clichéd phrases. The articles in this book are intended to avoid those pitfalls. The authors offer criticisms as well as praise. But they never rely on such time-worn catch-phrases as 'some vibration was apparent', and that greatest road-testing cliché of all, 'the controls fell readily to hand'.

Of the bikes under review, most are attainable rather than exotic. In other words, any reader could reasonably hope to own a similar machine at some time in the future. Most can be acquired for the aforementioned sums involving a few hundreds of pounds, although a Goldie in good condition will command far more than that, and haggling over a clean Vincent Rapide nowadays seems to start at around £3,000.

But certainly the parallel twins and most of the singles are accessible to enthusiasts. Perhaps these articles will guide intending owners to the machines that suit their particular requirements. And perhaps, too, there is room for later volumes in this series to cover the rarer machines of high pedigree, and more bikes from the vintage and post-vintage years up to 1939.

Below: Immediately recognisable, the Gold Star motor encapsulates a whole era.

Above: Another of Edward Turner's brainchildren, the Ariel Square Four in its last version.

Below: A thing of beauty is a joy forever, and the HRD is well worth a second look.

250 cc Aermacchi Ala Verde

by Val Ward

Aermacchi Ala Verde

It was thin, low and travelling very fast. Banking to what seemed impossible angles, it simply tore through a double S-bend with a clean staccato bark, and to my eternal chagrin someone else was on it. Before that silver-red dart was out of sight, I determined to savour the thrill first-hand. It has taken 17 years to make the dream reality, but the experience was worth waiting for. The Aermacchi Ala Verde is a gem.

That makes owner Tom Howitt very lucky, for even when generally available Aermacchis always were rare on British roads. The biggest thing against them was price. Great caution tempered keen interest: to English eyes, Italian cc's looked uncomfortably expensive. Sadly for the hopes of brave entrepreneurs, many potential buyers, declining to gamble on an unknown quantity, played safe and bought cheaper machines. In this country Aermacchi sales were comparatively few.

One-time importer Syd Lawton reckons that in the five or six years they were on the UK market little more than 100 Aermacchis came here. Consider the alternatives then available. In 1961 a new Ala Verde cost £259 — £50 to £70 more than most other sports 250s made in this country. The fact that the Aermacchi earned glowing praise from road-testers did nothing to persuade the vast majority of young riders at whom the Ala Verde was aimed to overlook the price differential.

Tom Howitt's immaculate Ala Verde, a 1962 66 x 72mm four-speeder, is a stunning performer. It is all the more impressive when one learns that the engine, rebuilt by tuner Francis Beart, is perfectly standard. The specification chart's claim of 18bhp at 6,750rpm looks nothing special by present-day values. But that reading, unusually, was taken at the rear wheel. When new, this bike would top 80mph.

Speed was Aermacchi's business from the start. In 1912 S A Nieuport Macchi was formed to produce aircraft, and in the early thirties a works competition plane set a speed record of 440mph. After the Second World War production switched to powered two-wheelers. Scooters preceded the first four-stroke Aermacchi, which appeared in 1956. This bike, the

Light, low and perfectly proportioned, the Ala Verde cut a distinctive if expensive dash in the early sixties.

Above: rakish boy racer front end is somewhat spoilt by the small 25/25W headlight and switchgear.

Left: short Ceriani suspension units attached to the tubular subframe provide a secure but choppy ride.

Chimera, set the pattern for the company's unmistakable road and racing machines with its almost horizontal cylinder, which designer Ing Alfredo Bianchi chose for its benefits of low centre of gravity and good roadholding.

The first sporting Aermacchis, made in 1957, introduced a line of distinctive names — Ala Bianchi (White Wing), Ala Azzurra (Light Blue Wing), Ala Rossa (Red Wing), and Ala Verde (Green Wing). All had the characteristic backbone frame comprising a single large-diameter top tube from steering head to swinging-arm pivot, and twin curved outriggers for short-travel rear suspension units.

Good torque and dashing lines to match the excellent top speed made the Ala Verde popular in Italy. Rugged and well made, this pushrod two-valver at 242lb dry was a featherweight alongside some contemporary 250s. The Varese factory, keen to develop export markets, refined the formula to create the Ala d'Oro (Golden Wing), a street-legal racer with lights. Weighing only 220lb it was made in both 175cc and 250cc forms: claimed maximum speeds were 93mph and 102mph respectively.

Lightness was the keynote to all Aermacchis. What little the Ala Verde has goes a long way: everything about it, from engine internals to handlebar levers, is just right with no unnecessary weight. British spares specialist Dick Linton says there were no particular troubles with the original design, though developments of the basic theme included a stronger caged-roller bearing for the big-end in 1963.

Lucid 'exploded' drawings in the official Aermacchi Harley-Davidson workshop manual show that the Ala Verde is uniformly robust. The pressed-up crankshaft has full disc flywheels and a reinforced streamlined connecting rod. Caged ball bearings support the left-side generator shaft and right-side primary drive shaft.

Electrical power comes from a four-pole, two-brush shunt generator, the armature assembly being driven by the flywheel shaft. To control charging of the six-volt, seven-amp battery, a regulator is tucked in a cavity between the tool boxes. Tom Howitt's bike now has a miniature Yuasa battery in place of the original Bosch, but ignition is still by coil.

A drawback with Aermacchi's method of construction is evident during major overhaul. Crankcases are split vertically and if big-end or serious gearbox trouble should occur, the engine must be removed from the frame and completely dismantled. Pullers are needed to fit/strip gear pinions and flywheel halves. But as the engine incorporates substantial primary drive gears, a strong clutch and a generous 3½-pint sump it will, with reasonable care, run for many thousands of miles needing little beyond periodic adjustment of contact breaker and valves.

Clamped to an iron barrel, a light-alloy cylinder head has a cast-in tunnel for pushrods worked by cams in the main engine casing. An underslung tube drains pressure-fed oil from valve gear to sump, where it passes through three filters for re-circulation by duplex pump; after 1964, the scavenge section of the pump was omitted. As the same oil serves the gearbox, Aermacchi recommend changing it every 1,000 miles.

Accessibility for general maintenance work is excellent. A two-bolt waterproof cover on the right-side engine case protects contact breaker and condenser. Unusually well-cooled, the cylinder head has two separate five-bolt rocker covers and a two-bolt tappet cover over simple screw-and-locknut adjusters; tappet clearance (cold) is .004in. The 14mm spark plug could not be easier to reach. Not that it gives trouble: indeed it is probably rusted in place.

Sound engineering and thoughtful touches also characterise many cycle parts. Those $7\frac{1}{2}$in ribbed brakes, with single leading shoes front and rear, might seem old-hat by current standards but they have surprising reserves of power. Because the cam-operating levers are both long and rigid, quite mild pressure on the controls quickly and effortlessly pulls down speed. To ensure long life for the rear fork bushes, the makers fitted grease nipples on the pivot housing.

The lion's share of the credit for a restoration job on the test machine that is only just short of flawless belongs to Michael Cleveland, a 33-year-old colliery electrician from Huthwaite, Nottinghamshire. Fascinated by this powerfully attractive lightweight, he spent several years collecting authentic parts to return a hacked-about machine to original specification and finished up with enough bits to make two and a half machines. Some components came from Syd Lawton of Lawton & Wilson, Southampton, who took over the UK concession on the death of the first importer, Bill Webster of Crewe, in the early sixties. Several cycle parts were particularly elusive.

Michael's repeated advertisements for missing bits drew many enquiries from other Aermacchi owners. He found they had the same problem: "All the people I heard from during my searches also needed parts—

A horizontal motor suspended from a spine frame are Aermacchi's unmistakable trade marks.

Plenty of space means the 18bhp (at the rear wheel) 246cc engine is admirably easy to work on.

All castings, and the engineering within them, are well up to the usual high Italian standard.

Aermacchi Ala Verde

I never did find another Ala Verde to catalogue specification in full working order. They seem to be very scarce in Britain." His main reason for selling the bike was that being a six-footer, he dwarfed it.

Though such parts as mudguards and tanks are now hard to obtain, vital bits for engines and gearboxes are still available and the works, renamed Cagiva Motor S.p.A., Via G Macchi 144 (Schiranna), 21100 Varese, will give advice. Dick Linton recommends factory sales manager Luigi Giacommetti: "He speaks very good English and is very helpful."

Brand-new components, however, are dear. Tom Howitt, who has the bones of a 28bhp Ala d'Oro, did well to acquire a stack of spares for £120, but a new front hub cost £90. Since getting the Ala Verde he has had craftsmen re-cover the seat, letter toolboxes in gold leaf and chrome some nuts and bolts. Externally, the only non-standard parts now are Borrani Record alloy rims, a seat hump and TT100s. The rocking pedal gear lever, sand-coloured handlebar grips, the CEV lighting system and switches are all authentic. Even the Silentium anti-blue snake on the exhaust pipe is correct.

The long struggle with the Aermacchi has been worthwhile: it is a little beauty. To be frank, that was the snag — for a rider of 5ft 10in or more, it does seem tiny. The only thing out of place on it during this test

Owner Tom Howitt puts the Ala Verde through its paces in its natural setting – a sunny country road.

was me: lumbering such a neat bike with Neanderthal galoshes and 170lb, a fair bit surplus to requirements, almost warrants a complaint to the RSPCA. The Aermacchi suffered in silence.

That was the bit it overdid. Tom, who knows the drill, turned on the single tap, flooded the carburettor and depressed the cold-start plunger on top. But I counted fourteen kicks on the rather awkward pedal before the engine fired. Surrounded by fresh air, cylinder head and barrel were slow to warm up. I set off gingerly but managed to stall it. With a fairly high bottom gear (15.4:1), the transmission demands coaxing for several yards before the clutch can take a break.

But little else about the Ala Verde requires much effort. All controls are light and it soon registers as everything a motorcycle should be — quick, lively, stable, taut, safe. Though 10 to 15mph behind modern sports 250s flat out, it can in other ways leave most of them standing. On tortuous roads, it's brilliant. Gripping like a racer, it sprints through gruelling swervery without a moment's hesitation, and nothing touches down when it is a long way from the vertical. Precise steering complements exceptionally good roadholding.

There's the puzzle: how do Italian manufacturers contrive to produce so many fine-handling bikes? Only once has an Italian machine's grasp disappointed me; to anyone bursting with curiosity the name will be sent under plain cover. The Ala Verde ranks with the best.

In the overweight eighties some happy trick of time seems to increase rather than diminish this bike's appeal. Peppy, flexible and beefy, the engine compensates for what feels like a fairly wide-ratio gearbox: I can understand now why later Aermacchis have five speeds.

Though gear lever movement is ponderous and the right boot must leave the footrest to reach it, engagement up or down the 'box is sweet and positive. My own inbuilt suspension, however, had to work overtime on rough byways to cancel out deficiencies in those squat, rather limited rear units. But grumbling is churlish. All Latin sports flyweights of this period were short on creature comforts. The Ala Verde, after all, was designed to let a rider know what his wheels are up to.

It was also meant to be — and is — light on the pocket. Thanks to the machine's small frontal area and compact style, a rider can draw 90 miles out of every gallon with ease — kid-glove tactics aren't necessary. And a beautiful 3¾-gallon tank makes it a long-distance express.

Hard to fault in daylight, the Aermacchi as things turned out saw no night-time action — probably just as well, in view of its elementary five-inch diameter headlamp and comical 25/25-watt main bulb. Some things are better left untried. I shall remember this Ala Verde for a long time — for all the right reasons.

Specification

1962 AERMACCHI ALA VERDE

ENGINE

Type	ohv single
Bore x stroke	66 x 72mm
Capacity	246cc
Compression ratio	8.5:1
Carburation	24mm Dell 'Orto
Bhp @ rpm	18 @ 6,750 (measured at rear wheel)
Electrical	6v battery and coil
Primary drive	helical gear
Clutch	multi-plate, wet
Gearbox	4 speed

DIMENSIONS

Frame	single backbone
Suspension	
(front)	Aermacchi/Ceriani two-way damped telescopic
(rear)	Ceriani damped struts
Tyres	
(front)	17 x 80/90 Dunlop TT100
(rear)	17 x 80/90 Dunlop TT100
Brakes	
(front)	7½in sls drum
(rear)	7½in sls drum
Wheelbase	52in
Seat height	30in
Ground clearance	5.75in
Dry weight	242lb
Fuel capacity	3.75gal

PERFORMANCE

Top speed	80mph (est)
Standing ¼ mile	18secs (est)
Fuel consumption	80mpg
Owner	Tom Howitt, Northants

600cc AJS Model 30

by Jerry Clayton

AJS Model 30

It was like riding a bicycle — something you never seem to forget. Pull in the clutch lever and swing the kickstart crank down a couple of times to clear the clutch plates, tickle the Amal Monobloc, retard the ignition just a shade, choke in and kick. Instantly, the AJS Model 30 600cc twin burst into life with a muted yet throaty burble. Ian Newman of Rafferty Newman grinned from ear to ear. So did I. In those milliseconds of time, we were like a couple of kids bubbling over as we were with sheer enthusiasm. Ian summed it up succinctly. "It's magic, isn't it?"

And it was. To be absolutely honest, I cannot recall having previously ridden an AJS or Matchless 'pure' twin. My era of road-testing commenced when AMC had begun to put Norton engines into Matchless frames, as in the Norton N15CS, during the sixties. Ian Newman's Model 30, identical to AMC's other breed, the Matchless G11, was in superb condition, and while I vaguely recalled something about his having greased the primary chain because of oil-tightness problems with the primary chaincase, the important aspect of the conversation leading up to this had been lost through one aperture and out of the other. It was destined to cause me a good deal of concern.

When the bikes were first introduced in 1956, it was obvious that the engine owed its heritage to the highly successful 500cc AJS Model 20 (Matchless G9), for the bore and stroke of the latter measured 66 x 72.8mm while the 600cc version, which was destined to run for a brief three-year span, measured 72 x 72.8mm — almost 'square'.

At the time of their introduction, the price was £260 0s 8d, but £50 of this was purchase tax. By the time the Newman AJS would have been sold in June 1957, the price had risen slightly to £280 4s 9d. Reflections on these figures brought forth an amusing little anecdote from Ian to the effect that apparently, you would buy an Ajay or a Matchless and then the dealer would add on 10d for a kickstart rubber! They were never supplied as standard.

The later 650cc engines, as I recall from youthful involvement with that era, suffered from heavy wear on cams and followers, but this may have been attributable to the sportier camshafts of the CSR models I knew. The problem was not a new one. The 500 engine went through three stages of development, the earliest of which suffered real trouble with very short cam followers.

All of which is surprising when we return to the 600, because the basic engine was designed specifically to withstand higher revs. In designing the 500 twin, AMC opted for a unique feature, namely the fitting of a central main bearing to obviate 'whirling'. The argument was simple. The air-cooling of two parallel

The Model 30 was produced for only three years, after which the 600cc twin became a full 650.

A typically British handlebar layout – the steering damper does not iron out shake completely.

After the famous but leaky Jampot, AMC used these Girling type dampers with special clevis fittings.

cylinders dictated that they had to be a certain distance apart to accommodate cooling fins, and therefore the fitting of a central shell bearing meant that the crankshaft would have to be no longer. The torque setting on this was critical, being in the region of just 18 psi. Quite apart from these considerations, it meant in turn that if the central bearing was positively fed between the two crank throws, then the shell bearing big ends would receive an equal supply of lubricant. The cast iron barrels and alloy heads were separate castings used for both the 500 and 600cc models and obviously, the cast iron crankshaft carried two flywheels with the centre bearing in between.

Most contemporaries used ball or roller bearing mains (AMC opted for rollers with the 20, 30, G9 and G11 models) but they also tended to go for tappets to follow cam profiles. AMC designers decided on short cam followers which pivoted on a pin and carried pushrod locating cups on their backs. It was simply another way to reduce reciprocating weight, and the camshafts themselves ran in three phosphor bronze bushes. At the top end of the motor, the rocker arms carried no additional reciprocating weight such as an adjusting screw and locknut, any tolerance being adjusted by means of an eccentric rocker spindle.

Timing gear pinions moved away from some latter-day thinking, which would slim down such items to trim weight and drag. On the AMC twins these pinions were 9/16in wide! Hiduminium RR56 light alloy con-rods were of substantial 'I' section and the factory claimed at one time that the rods could be expected to fail at the gudgeon pin eye, but added the corollary that this could be anticipated only after the engine had been run flat out for 50 years! The same rods were used in the 500, 600 and 650 versions — with the 650 the crank throws were changed. Two separate oil pumps were used on the engines, gear types carried within a light alloy casting inside the timing chest and driven via slotted ends on each camshaft. At peak rpm, these pumped 24 gallons of lubricant an hour.

It may have seemed a slightly archaic practice to some, but the retention of manual advance and retard control made sense at AMC, where they believed that automatic advance/retard units cancelled out their usefulness when they were probably most needed — in cold start situations. The general feeling was that a rider would become accustomed to the best manual setting for starting this machine under varying conditions. Details like this made it clear that the AJS Model 30 and Matchless GII were designed as semi-sporting twins, owing more than a large slice of their construction not only to the G9 and Model 20 but also to the Matchless G45 500cc racing twins. They became, during their era, accepted transport for clubmen.

Which brings us back to the present. Ian Newman's Model 30 had been owned previously by an enthusiast in his fifties, who had sold the bike just two years beforehand. And his pride of ownership certainly showed. There were some, dare I say it without sounding effeminate, lovely touches. Maybe 'loving touches' would be a more accurate description, but whoever he is he deserves, as Ian will readily admit, most of the credit for the machine's condition. For example, where some of the wiring was exposed on the left hand side of the bike, it had been carefully sheathed in plastic tubing. There were tools in the toolbox on the left hand side, carefully wrapped in a wallet and surrounded with a piece of cloth, and all the controls were silky smooth to the degree that operating them made one feel like some kind of interloper. Perhaps it's a difficult feeling to get across, but I trust that erstwhile owner will read these lines and at least know that his efforts were appreciated. But such glowing thoughts only served to increase that concern I mentioned earlier.

After riding the bike home I rang a fellow enhusiast with a view to chewing the fat, knowing that he was something by way of an authority on the AMC marques, which I am not. "1957 you say, Model 30? I bet there's oil pouring out of the drive side breather, yes sir, even with just on 40,000 miles on the clock. They all had that wear out y'know, and that blasted primary chaincase was a devil to seal properly".

They're not original equipment but the tools reveal a sensible concern for roadside emergencies.

Returning the telephone to its cradle, I rushed into the garage. No, the floor was absolutely spotless. Breathing a sigh of happy relief and muttering "Huh, what does he know?" I returned to try and work out my two-piece jigsaw puzzle. The floor remained spotless for a further day, and then all hell broke loose.

Lying canted on its prop stand, the Ajay proceeded to drop frightening quantities of oil. I thought of all the loving care which had previously been bestowed on it and felt ghastly. Never in the running for a 'Mechanic of the Year' award, I stood her on the centre stand and hoped the flapper valve in the end of the crankshaft might heal itself overnight!

In fact, using the prop stand in all probability helped the situation. What happens is that once the breather valve starts to go the oil flinger inside the bearing can't do its job and the primary case fills up. The oil level in the right hand side oil tank drops correspondingly. It was on the last few miles back to Rafferty Newmans' in Dean Road, Bitterne, Southampton, that the clutch at last started to slip slightly because of all the oil. And only on returning the bike did I discover that Ian had found the chaincase full when he had been giving it the once-over before I took delivery. The Ajay's breather valve problem meant that a fairly careful watch had to be kept on the oil level in the tank, and the excess drawn off from the chaincase when expedient and thrown away.

But 21 years after it first ran, the Model 30 still provided more than happy motoring, and the strangest feeling of all was not having to continually stop for petrol. That may sound a little cock-eyed, but I filled the bike with petrol in Southampton and then covered 180 miles on just 2.6 gallons — a consumption figure of 69mpg. Admittedly, along the B road to Corhampton and northwards along the A32 to Alton I simply enjoyed the ride, but Ian had confessed to taking the bike up to 85mph, so I stuck at a steady 70 whenever possible. The ride brought back firm memories of the 60mpg I achieved from my old T'Bird up to the Isle of Man and back in 1963.

Handling with the single downtube frame cannot be classed as exemplary by modern day standards. The downtube splits under the engine and runs around to form the rear triangular loop across which, just behind the gearbox, a rectangular box section cross member of substantial proportions raises vertically and takes the swinging arm spindle. Almost traditionally, for the period, this is joined by an upright seat pillar which drops down from the saddle nose where it is joined by the single top tube rail under the tank (suitably braced at the headstock) and

More powerful than the 500cc version, sweeter and less troublesome than the 650, this engine hits the golden mean. Sadly it was not in production for many years.

the double loop, the latter having supplied anchor points for the top of the rear suspension units. The rear suspension units were not of the 'jampot' variety — great fat affairs from which the AJS and Matchless Owners' club magazine gets its title — but more like standard Girlings. They featured a clevis fitting at their lower end specially made for AMC by Girling, and carried three pre-load settings.

The biggest surprise came with the potency of the AMC 7in brakes — standard for many years with a lining width of just $\frac{7}{8}$in for a total lining area of $23\frac{1}{2}$sq in. The front brake in particular made no bones about arresting the Ajay's 400-odd lb (dry weight is listed as 396lb) and would easily compress the patented Teledraulic front forks, causing the tyre to squeal.

We hear and read so much about excessive tyre wear these days that it's pleasant to report that both the Avon tyres (a 3.25 x 19 Speedmaster ribbed on the front and a 3.50 x 19 SM Mk2 patterned cover on the rear) gave no real problems on wet or dry roads and still appeared set for several thousand miles. The main restriction I discovered on left hand corners was the centre stand peg — but nothing grounded as far as I was prepared to lean into right handers on such a bike.

The Model 30's handling showed its weakness when the bike was asked to change line rapidly. A

Well suspended and not too heavy, the Ajay still shakes its head when asked to change line rapidly.

distinctive shaking of the steering head would accompany this manoeuvre. Tightening and loosening the black steering damper knob which runs down through the head produced little effect either way — it's just an inherent fault.

The AMC gearbox with its 13.9, 8.9, 6.9, and 5.3:1 ratios was really superb, and it's small wonder that many special builders still insist on using it. Gearchange is on the right, naturally, and even without the message from a modern neutral indicator light, it was easy to find neutral. Indeed, if one applied too little pressure when changing from first into second, the box would hang up in neutral (which, I confess, happened to me twice). The clutch action, like all the controls, was really sweet with just a hint of 'servo' on take-up.

We all thought that moving on from six-volt to 12-volt lighting was a good idea. It must be, at least from the viewpoint of availability of bulbs, but riding the Model 30 at night proved the lie, so to speak, for the 30/24 watt six-volt headlamp gave a terrific spread and was certainly good enough for 60-65mph cruising. Obviously, Lucas headlamp reflectors must take a fair amount of the credit, for I've experienced far worse lighting on modern 12-volt machines with bigger wattage bulbs.

Comfort on the AJS was pretty good, marred only by a little mid-range vibration from the engine. Brake and clutch adjustment could be taken up at the levers, and I found that if a little retard was used when climbing long gradients or trundling along in heavy traffic, the motor's response was just that much sweeter, I can see AMC's viewpoint here, for you do have the option of playing with the advance/retard lever.

Saddle height at a shade over 31in and broad with it meant that handling the bike could be a struggle for a lady, but that's all. Apart from delivering a fairly hefty swing on the right hand mounted kickstarter, there would be no other snags.

All told, it's no wonder to me that the Model 30 and the Matchless G11 gained the popularity they did. Quite by chance almost, the factory had hit on 'square' dimensions for a very strong, free-revving engine. If the problem with the oil breather had been cured and the later type alloy chaincase fitted the bikes may well have gone on for many more years. As it was, they appeared for three years only — 1956 to '58 — before being superseded by the Model 31 and the Matchless G12, both of which, in 1959, had CSR variants. The dimensions changed again to 72 x 79.3mm bore and stroke although the barrels, heads and cranks were basically the same. But a batch of new problems started. That is not to say that all the bigger AMC bikes were beset with malfunctions, yet somehow the AJS Model 30 and the Matchless G11 600s seem, in the light of this test, to have got it just right.

Specification

600cc AJS MODEL 30

ENGINE

Type	**ohv parallel twin**
Bore x stroke	**72 x 72.8mm**
Capacity	**592cc**
Compression ratio	**7.5:1**
Carburation	**Amal Monobloc 376/78**
Bhp @ rpm	**32 at 6,700rpm**
Primary drive	**chain**
Clutch	**multi-plate, wet**
Gearbox	**4 speed**
Electrical system	**Lucas magneto and 6v. 60w dynamo**
Lighting	**30/24w headlamp**

DIMENSIONS

Wheelbase	**55.25in**
Seat height	**31.5in**
Ground clearance	**5.5in**
Kerb weight	**421lb (inc 1gal fuel)**
Fuel capacity	**3.75gal**
Tyres	
(front)	**3.25 x 19 Avon Speedmaster**
(rear)	**3.50 x 19 Avon SM Mk II**
Brakes	
(front)	**7in**
(rear)	**7in**

PERFORMANCE

Top speed	**90mph (approx)**
Standing ¼ mile	**17secs (approx)**
Fuel consumption	**69mpg**
Braking distance	
from 30mph	**29ft**
from 60mph	**N/A**
Owner	**Ian Newman, Rafferty Newman, Southampton.**

250cc Ambassador Super S

by Val Ward

250cc Ambassador

Good bikes don't always get the credit they deserve. For proof, look at the Ambassador Super S. When this two-fifty first appeared, there was a lot to recommend it. Smart, well thought out and nicely made, it had a finish way above average and its general performance put it ahead of most contemporaries. Yet strangely its popularity was never blinding.

The reason may be that it was a half-and-half design — semi orthodox roadster, semi boxed-in glimpse of the future. While Ariel's 1958 Leader, revolutionary throughout, was so fully enclosed that a side view gave no hint of its power unit, the Ambassador was only partly faired and left its Villiers 2T engine out in the open. Like other bold makers before them, Ambassadors tried to reconcile warring options when they updated their range in the late fifties, and certainly their new-for-1959 two-stroke twin had panache. Attractive styling and smooth lines complemented brisk acceleration, modest thirst, a very sweet gearbox and a top speed of just over 70mph to make the Super S perhaps the best of Britain's home-grown two-fifties.

Strong on value for money, Ambassadors were unfortunately rather weak on publicity. Though Normans got a wonderful boost when Derek Minter demonstrated their B4 Sports Twin at Brands Hatch, Ambassadors failed to make the most of their sparkling creation in the magazine of the time. After a four-year run and several marketing jolts, manufacture of this clean-living lightweight from the factory at Ascot in Berkshire ceased. For the Super S, however, that wasn't the end of the road for, moved to DMWs at Sedgley in Worcestershire, Ambassadors survived 'til 1965 when the new owners' other interests in the motorcycle field — chiefly hub, brake and fork development — stopped bike production.

The Ambassador story at Ascot began in January 1947. Their first production roadster was a rigid-framed 200cc single, powered by the ubiquitous

Practical German influence is seen in the deeply valanced mudguards and sensible ancillary equipment.

Workhorse of many a bike, the Villiers 2T unit provides adequate and reliable power.

Four gears allow the Ambassador to cover ground at a respectable, unstressed rate of knots.

Villiers 5E engine with bolted-up gearbox and shown in 1948 at Earls Court — Britain's first postwar Show. Steady development and careful expansion over the next few years led in 1953 to the SS Supreme which, unusually for the day, had electric starting. For 1954 Ambassador took on a profitable sideline: they agreed to import Zundapps whose teutonic influence was evident in some of the later British-built two-strokes. For instance, mudguards grew deep valances, petrol tank caps became kingsize and generous seven-inch headlamps were standardised.

In 1957 Ambassador offered seven different bikes ranging in size from a 150cc Villiers single, the Popular, to the pride of the line, the 249cc twin-cylinder Supreme. A fully-equipped four-speeder, it was plush and quite energetic and, customer feedback being favourable, Ambassadors re-cast it to enter the luxury class with a flourish. Kaye Don's Ascot team may not have got everything right and today their 1959 blueprint for a de luxe roadster with zip seems dated, but it was undoubtedly attractive then. On showroom floors from Land's End to John o' Groats the Super S looked competitive and exerted strong appeal.

At £193 give or take a few shillings, the Ambassador stood out as a neatly-proportioned variation on the two-stroke twin theme. Panther's Model 35, a rather unhappy blend of Earles-type front fork, awkward frame and Villiers 2T engine, did nothing for the reputation of the Yorkshire marque, while the leading-link Armstrong forks on Sun's Overlander and Norman's B4 pegged them back in the styling stakes as did Greeves' similar suspension. Other companies' efforts to unite beauty and function round a 2T centre are perhaps best forgotten: most looked odd and some were terrible.

Balance could well have been the Ascot firm's watchword. Off its main stand, cushioned on wide 17-inch tyres and ready to go the Ambassador was a handsome treat in a period of ugly and unsatisfactory performers. In action its appeal rose dramatically for zestful behaviour proved it was a wolf in sheep's clothing.

Flung into cruel bends, it exhibited sports-type roadholding to confound a rider who might think such a cultured appearance denoted flabby manners. Taut steering was another welcome shock from this sedate-looking tourer, though admittedly choppy going caned the undamped teles, which rapid braking could also embarrass. There was, however, little more to fault. Given a hard time in traffic jams, the clutch might complain and still-air conditions at heat-wave temperatures on slow stuff could upset carburation, yet everything else held up and backyard maintenance was free of snags for the man who liked to do it himself.

Fred Hibbert, a telephonist from Buxton, needs no persuading of the Ambassador's worth. He first realised he was on to a good thing with the Berkshire marque in 1954 when he bought a new 197cc Embassy with the Villiers 8E motor — "a superb machine", says Fred. He kept it for six years and during 60,000 miles in his hands it gave little trouble. The quality finish also impressed Fred who recalls that when he sold the bike in 1960 the paint and chrome were still excellent. So after disappointing adventures with other British two-strokes, among them a James Captain, a Greeves Sports Twin, a Francis Barnett Falcon and a 2T Cotton he decided to concentrate on Ambassadors.

Today a detailed and still growing knowledge of Ambassadors makes Fred one of the marque's foremost specialists, and a peep at his cache of spares shows just how deep his one-make commitment

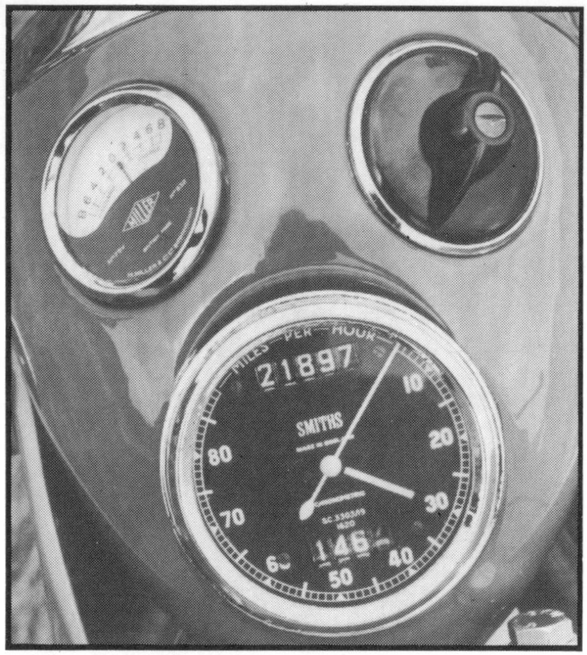

Basic but functional instruments adorn the Super S's headlamp nacelle.

Single downtube frame is sturdy enough to allow the Ambassador to be driven hard round corners.

All that sheet metal gives the machine an elegantly dated appearance.

runs. In a big shed awaiting either overhaul or nothing more difficult than reassembly are frames, suspension units, wheels and whole engines including one that is virtually new.

"There is no Ambassador owners club — I suppose I am the nearest thing to that," says Fred who will gladly advise on bikes, colour schemes, wiring diagrams and parts. His eventual aim is to have a totally authentic example of every model Ambassadors produced. At the moment he has six Ambassadors — four to Super S specification, a 1954 225cc Supreme with the lusty single-cylinder unit, and a 1961 Electra which is distinguished from kickstart versions of the 2T unit by a fatter engine case for the Siba Dynastart system. His main interest, however, is the Super S and the best in his collection offers a graphic reminder of just what can be achieved with limited resources.

At ten paces its outward appearance is textbook and if scrutiny from ten inches reveals a finish below Rolls-Royce standard, remember it was all done by hand-held brush. The result of Fred's careful work is faithful evocation of 1960 motorcycling, though much effort was needed to put his showpiece Super S back to catalogue trim.

Acquired in Halifax nine years ago, it was anything but original when he first saw it, having been cafe racerised with alloy guards and dropped 'bars, and

A happy tester swinging one of his favourite bikes along a pleasant country road.

many enquiries were made before he rounded up missing components to make it standard again. One side of the curvaceous front mudguard, obtained secondhand, had to be beaten out but there was better luck with other used parts. Former Ambassador agents Davies Brothers of Chester supplied the correct silencers, Smiths of Bakewell the full rear chaincase and handlebar cover, Dave Crouch of Classic Bikes in Herstmonceux both rear panels and DMWs a brand-new headlamp rim, sealed beam unit, and exhaust pipes.

Other details that recall one aspect of life on two wheels twenty-one years ago include tiny protective pads for front fork sliders, the internal springs being adjustable for load, a 95mph Smiths speedometer with resettable trip mileage recorder, twin-tone horns in side covers, a stout lifting handle-cum-grabrail behind the dualseat and Ambassador's distinctive "Polymist" lacquer for engine cases. Unable to get ex-works paint, Fred found Dulux Coach Finish in signal red almost identical, and to beat rust used Finnigan's Hammerite with a tough undercoat on other fittings.

Though Fred says crankshafts can wilt after prolonged use, no such trouble arose in this test, the only complaint being a bout of ignition hiccups from the non-standard NGK plugs below 35mph when the Super S was trapped behind a groaning lorry on a tortuous climb. Free of double white lines and other restrictions, the Ambassador zoomed into the distance with a healthy purr from the tailpipes time and again, and when it had to stop quickly to avoid a car whose driver misjudged its speed of approach the single-leading-shoe Albions, with a rod to beef up the one behind, responded eagerly and with assurance.

Rapid pick-up over 30mph in second and third — 10.9:1 and 7.6:1 respectively in this nifty 'box — compensated for some mechanical jangling and woolly transmission when dawdling, and useful handling encouraged trust in tight corners. Giving 110mpg on four-star at 30mph, the Ambassador starts promptly, revs cleanly and demands no special technique to keep its engine sharp for many thousands of miles. Only periodic de-coking, which is dead easy on this two-stroke, is needed since modern lubricants — Fred favours Bel-Ray at 30-to-1 — inhibit fall-out deposits.

The Ambassador, having sensible lights, sturdy bones and proven longevity, goes on delivering exhilaration long after faster, more highly-tuned bikes have deteriorated to an unacceptable level. Since the intervening years have shown no major weaknesses, the conclusion must be that the Super S was deliberately understressed at the drawing-board stage.

I'm glad to have had this opportunity to re-assess it in the light of interim developments. But I have to admit I expected it to be as impressive as it is — I had a new one.

Specification

1960 AMBASSADOR SUPER S

ENGINE

Type	two-stroke twin
Bore & stroke	50 x 63.5mm
Capacity	249cc
Compression ratio	8.2:1
Carburettor	Villiers 22mm
Bhp @ rpm	15 @ 5,500
Electrical	6-volt. Flywheel magneto with twin h.t. coils
Primary drive	single-row chain in oilbath
Clutch	wet multi plate
Gearbox	4-speed, foot change

DIMENSIONS

Frame	tubular
Suspension	
(front)	undamped telescopic
(rear)	Girling 3-position spring units, with hydraulic damping
Tyres	
(front)	3.25 x 17in Dunlop ribbed
(rear)	3.25 x 17in Dunlop studded
Brakes	
(front)	Albion 7in sls drum
(rear)	Albion 7in sls drum
Wheelbase	51in
Seat height	30in
Ground clearance	6½in
Weight	310lb
Fuel capacity	3.5gal

PERFORMANCE

Top speed	71mph
Standing start ¼ mile	19secs (est)
Fuel consumption	
(petroil)	70mpg
Owner	Fred Hibbert, Buxton, Derbyshire.

250cc Ariel Arrow

by Jerry Clayton

Ariel Arrow

The way in which this road test finally reached fruition could have taken thousands of words to explain. But to cut your agony short, let me simply state that for what was once such a popular machine, strangely few Arrows can be seen on British roads today when compared with such ubiquitous iron as Triumph and BSA twins.

However, at the time I was asked to find one I had by pure coincidence spent almost a week with a Golden Arrow — the sports model — that was in almost pristine condition. The bike was owned by a new motorcycling convert in South London, John Doyle, who had finally succumbed to endless years of badgering by yours truly to try two wheels. My experiences with his bike had been unusual, to say the least.

Unfortunately John, with uncharacteristic exuberance, ran out of road — that's probably kinder than saying he was going too fast — and the bike's right hand side was badly chamfered in the process. The owner was luckier, and escaped with a chipped ankle. But with the unexpected commissioning of this test, my 'unusual experience' with the Arrow took on a new meaning — I now had to locate another one. The task wasn't to be as easy as I had expected.

For those of you who can recall, as I do, the early sixties, the fact that the Arrow is now a rarity might come as something of a shock. Certainly, I hadn't given the problem much thought while I'd been involved with John Doyle's bike. But now I followed the trail of another Arrow from the police station at Bexhill, to Mr Weston at Heathfield Motor Cycles in Sussex (they carry quite a few Ariel spares), to ex-owner Roy Lesson at Hailsham, and finally to the machine's present owner in Lower Willingdon, near Eastbourne, John Stretton. Basically original, the Stretton Arrow had inevitably suffered the rigours of 13 years of use, losing along the way its right hand engine cover, the air cleaner hose and the original seat.

Anyway, I digress, but I hope the point is made that it does seem as though there are not too many Arrows about these days — although I must admit I've noticed a few Leaders since being involved in this test venture. The Leader, a fully enclosed, touring version of the Ariel twin-cylinder two-stroke theme was launched in 1958, and was designed by Val Page, one of the most brilliant and versatile engineers in the history of the British industry, who sadly died recently at the age of 86.

The bike was distinctly unorthodox, for it featured trailing link front forks, and the engine was slung beneath the 20-gauge pressed-steel beam frame. The fuel tank resided under the seat and the dummy 'tank' housed a tool tray which, when removed, uncovered

Using a compression ratio of 10:1 the square dimensioned two stroke motor puts out a useful 20bhp at 6500rpm.

Full enclosure of chain and damper was derived from the Arrow's touring predecessor, the Leader.

electrical components such as the rectifier and the coils. Honda Gold Wing, you were scooped.

The Leader had so much going for it, especially with regard to road-holding, that the next step was pure logic — a sporting version duly dubbed the Arrow by Selly Oak. Even today, that road-holding is exemplary. The 1964 Arrow I rode was suffering slightly from worn rear shock absorbers — they are not adjustable for pre-load, incidentally — and the front forks appeared to have some lateral movement probably caused by worn bushes. These faults wouldn't have been apparent when the bike was new.Even so, it was easy to appreciate why people used to get so hooked on Arrow handling. With 16-in wheels, the whole plot sits low to start with, and the centre of gravity is further kept down by the underslung engine and the fuel housed under the seat.

The design of the beam frame is such that the loads imposed run parallel to the walls, and it has to be fairly deep near the steering head to cope with braking loads. The Ariel design gives an extremely high degree of torsional stiffness which, in all probability, would have been improved only marginally by the use of a box section swinging arm at the rear. The trailing link front forks, with dampers and springs running up inside the legs, took everything in their stride, and, at least when the units were new, fast bumpy bends would be smoothed out and the bike would remain rock steady.

But quite apart from the Ariel factory's own problems, the biggest marketing bugbear the Arrow and Leader had to overcome at that time was the motorcycling movement's peculiarly insular feelings about anything unconventional. It was therefore something of a boon to the factory when, in 1960, the government restricted all learner riders to machines of 250cc or under.

Now the novice motorcyclist of those days was less set in his ways than dyed in-the-wool enthusiasts who had been nurtured on conventionally-framed four-strokes. An advertisement in the June 16, 1960, issue of *Motor Cycling* carried the kind of weight that might woo learner riders to the inherent virtues of the Arrow. Placed by the giant dealers, King's of Oxford, it announced that an Ariel Arrow "practically the same as you can buy for £167 13s 5d (£167.67p) lapped the Isle of Man Mountain TT course at 80.17mph". The fact that the race report in the magazine more correctly listed rider Mike O'Rourke's average *race* speed as 80.18mph during his seventh place in the 250cc Lightweight race is splitting hairs, but suffice to say that the Arrow finished ahead of NSUs, Bianchis and Ducatis. The cheers that greeted O'Rourke as he crossed the line on June 13, and again the same evening at the Villa Marina prize-giving ceremony, were just rewards for an 'underdog' ride on a roadster-based two-stroke with piston-port induction racing against specialist machinery. The Arrow had indeed arrived.

And while it couldn't be maintained that the Herman Meier-tuned engine of O'Rourke's bike was anything like standard, it's significant that in October of that year, the compression ratio of the Arrow's 'square' 54 x 54mm engine was raised from 8.25 to 10:1. New oval con rods were fitted, and the carburettor was changed from an Amal 375/33 to a 376/277, which meant that the choke size went up from 7/8in to 1-1/16in, while the main jet was increased from 140 to 230. On paper at least, the changes gave an extra four bhp (up to 20 at 6,500rpm) at 500 fewer revs, but on the road the difference was startling. It was not uncommon to see packs of riders mounted on Triumphs, Nortons, Ajays, Enfields and the like thundering off to their local haunts on summer evenings with, perhaps slightly behind, another couple of riders, heads down, humping along in the upper seventies with that tell-tale swirl of blue two-stroke haze spiralling behind. Nine times out of ten, 'L' plates would be taped over the deeply valanced front mudguards of the pursuing Arrows, indicating that their riders were fledglings learning to fly!

So, when we return to the present day and get the chance to ride a Golden Arrow, as the sports version of October 1960 eventually became, it comes as something of a shock to realise how the world has passed it by — on two counts.

Firstly, while I've stressed the qualities of the beam frame's structure and torsional ability in keeping the Arrow's wheels pointing in the same direction under varying circumstances and over differing road surfaces, no other manufacturer has taken up development in this direction.

Secondly, riding the bike today reminded me just how much sophistication the Japanese have introduced into two-strokes. The Arrow engine as ridden — and bear in mind its age and the careless treatment it may have been subjected to — was fairly noisy on John Doyle's bike. There seemed a fair amount of clatter and ignition resonance through the separate alloy cylinder heads, and the noise emitted by the exhaust was slightly coarser than expected.

Despite the bike's age it was easy enough to start, and everything in this department seemed as standard. The ignition key fits into a switch on the right of the headlamp shell, and with the fuel switched on, the choke near the petrol tap is pulled out. Only once did it over-choke in warm weather, and it was found that it would fire up even more easily with just half the choke engaged. A petroil ratio of 25:1 was used on the test machine, but, as revealed later, was probably too rich a blend.

Gear changing through a right hand lever with a one up, three down, pattern was notchy, and the operation of the three-plate clutch was deceptively stiff.

Despite the worn items on the test bike, the handling remained first rate. The only snag was a weak centre stand spring, which allowed the stand to flutter up and down on bumpy surfaces and make contact with the road. But the biggest snag of all, and one which I believe was also experienced when the bikes were first tested years ago, was the soggy feeling of the rather puny 6in front brake. I learned later that by slackening the fulcrum adjusting bolts and applying either the front lever or rear pedal while retightening,

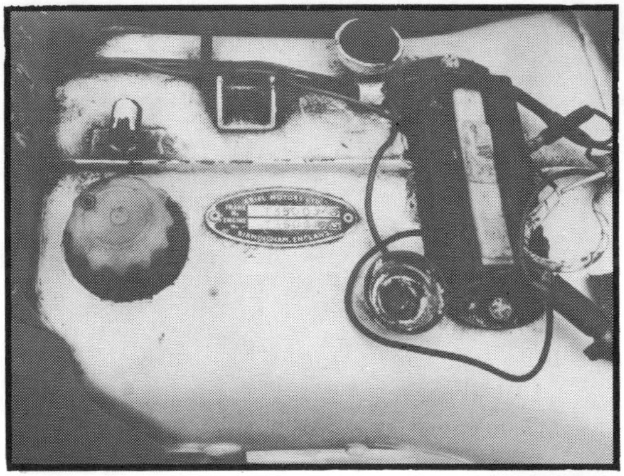

Left: real fuel tank is situated under the seat. Dummy tank houses tool tray and electrics.

Above: drawing reveals clearly the beam frame – a daring innovation – made up from pressed steel.

Ariel Arrow

Below: the piston ported twin in all its glory. Note the cast central support – cum – induction channel.

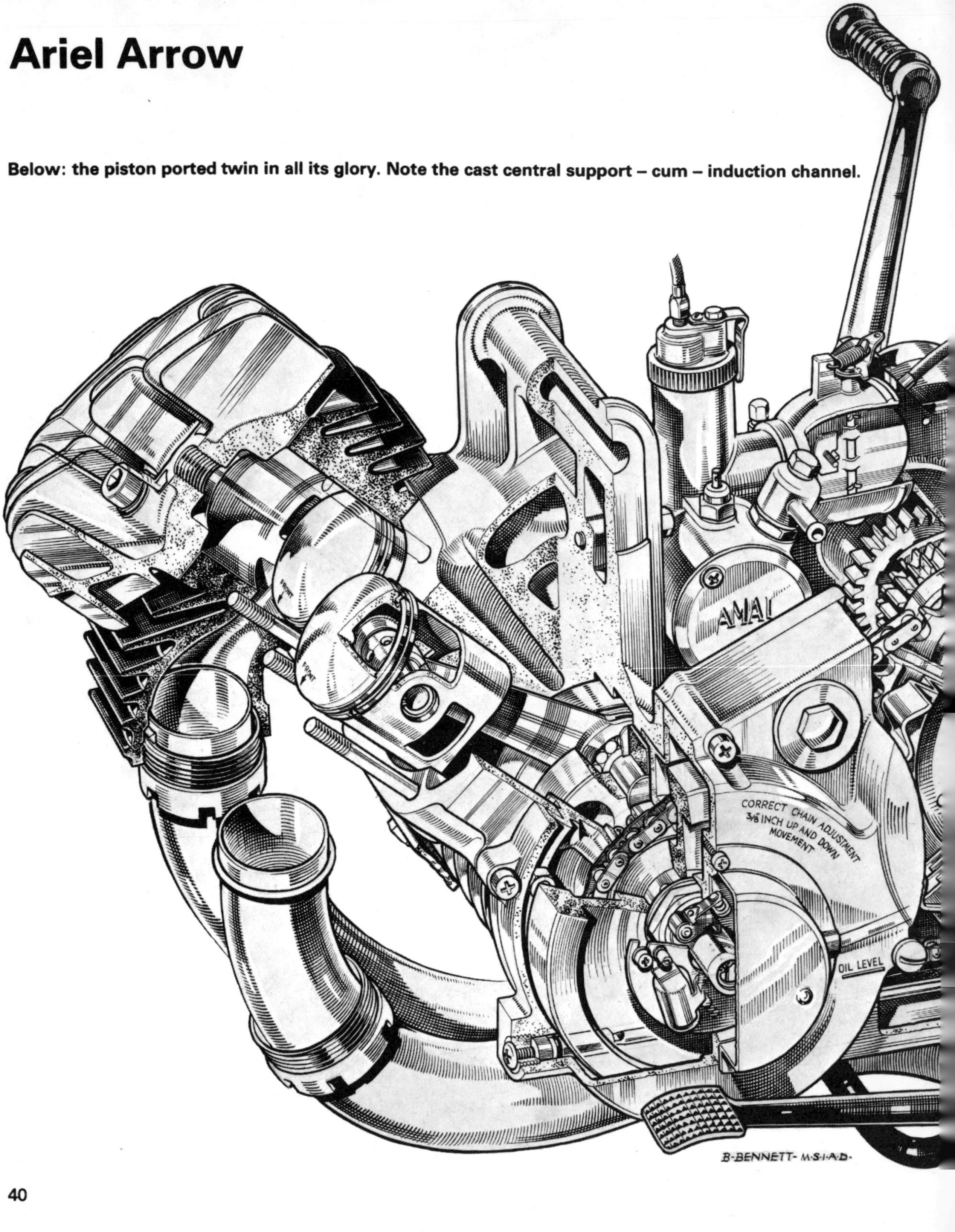

Above: Ace bars came as standard. Instrumentation is functional rather than comprehensive.

optimum lining area can be brought into contact with the hub. Even so, a poor front brake appears to be the norm on Arrows.

The forks are unusual in that the legs containing the dampers and their springs only extend up as far as the cup-and-cones steering head, the handlebars being mounted on the central steering column, and there is no top yoke. The rod operating the 6in rear brake emerges on the right hand side of the bike from the left foot-operated pedal. The fully enclosed rear chain is lubricated from the primary chaincase — a first rate scheme — and this is on the left, hence the brake arrangement. The rear anchor proved much harsher than the front unit in operation, incidentally.

Electrics on the Arrow were six volt, which wouldn't matter so much except that the diameter of the 24/30-watt front headlamp is only six inches, on a machine capable of reaching nearly 80mph! Needless to say, night riding was conducted with due caution. It was at night that an indicated 50 to 55mph in top gear was found to give the most satisfying ride. At that speed the Arrow just burbled along, with all the harshness of hard acceleration forgotten. Speeds in the gears, as indicated on the somewhat small speedometer which tended to run haywire at readings over 70mph, were just under 20mph in first, 40mph in second, 55 in third, and somewhere in the upper 70s in top.

Originally fitted with Dunlop whitewall tyres, the wheels of John Doyle's bike were shod with Czechoslovakian Barums. In contrast, John Stretton's bike was using the combination of an Avon Speedmaster and an Avon SM Mk 2. The Arrow's rear wheel is quickly detachable after attention to only three bolts, when removal leaves the chain undisturbed. Original equipment on the Golden Arrow included 'ace' bars and a flyscreen which clipped to them. The test bike had neither, being fitted with semi-straight bars and lacking the screen.

There are varying accounts of fuel consumption figures on the Ariel two-strokes, but this can probably be explained by the differing carburettor choke sizes on the early models and those on the far more popular later models that ran from 1960 until 1966,

16 inch wheels, low centre of gravity, leading link forks and a stiff frame combine to give good handling.

when production ceased. Some owners of Leaders claim around 80mpg, but consumption figures closer to 50mpg are more likely on the Arrow. With a three-gallon tank, however, this will be acceptable to most owners.

In a recent issue of *Motor Cycle News* there were just two Arrows on offer in the classified ads pages. One was a 1962 model with loads of spares that was going for £165, and the other was a 1960 version, available at £87. John Stretton paid £170 for his 1965 Arrow, and was offered £240 just a fortnight later.

Perhaps, too, modern two-stroke oils have advanced sufficiently over the years for John to mix his petroil in a 32:1 ratio quite happily. I've since discovered that even in the Leader/Arrow handbook, a ratio of 24:1 was recommended with some types of two-stroke oil, while 32:1 was advised for other lubricants.

On the question of spare parts, John Stretton needed a stator plate for his generator and got one off the shelf at John Groombridge Motorcycles in Sussex on an exchange deal! But as with most obsolete machinery, it can be wise for riders to join the appropriate owners' club. Membership of the Ariel Owners' Club costs only £2.50 a year (the secretary is John Mortimer, 75 Sebright Road, Barnet, Herts), and different officials specialise in looking after spares supplies for the various Ariel models. Engine components for the two-strokes are in reasonable supply, although items such as panels, boxes and screens for the Leader bodywork are becoming more difficult to locate. For Leader and Arrow riders in the Midlands, Bob Joyner and Son at Warley, West Midlands, is another source of parts.

There could well be a resurgence of interest in these bikes, which represent the last fling of a once great factory — apart from the disastrous Ariel-3 three-wheeled moped produced by BSA in more recent times. I didn't like at the time the bikes were being produced the use of cross-head bolts and the frame and engine, but that is personal taste. On test, I found too that the coils are not readily accessible and that to actually reach them, the headlamp has to be removed. Access to the rectifier, on the other hand, is through the aperture behind the left-hand 'tank' badge. Owners could probably do well to re-locate the coils inside the 'tank' so that they are accessible after the toolbox is removed.

I found, too, that the centre stand played havoc with the sole of my right boot as I manhandled the bike onto the stand. Even so, because it was such an unconventional model, beloved by youth a decade and a half ago, the Ariel Arrow takes on a character all its own. It won't hold a modern Yamaha or Suzuki 250 on acceleration, but just wait for the next corner to prove a point!

Specification

250cc ARIEL ARROW

ENGINE

Type	two-stroke twin
Bore and stroke	54 x 54mm
Capacity	249cc
Compression ratio	8.25:1 pre-1960; 10.0:1 from 1960
Carburation	Amal 7/8in pre-1960; Amal 1.1/16in from 1960
Bhp @ Rpm	16 @ 7000 pre-1960; 20 @ 6500 from 1960
Primary drive	single row chain
Clutch	multi-plate, wet
Gearbox	4 speed
Electrical system	Lucas 6 volt 50 watt generator, battery and coil ignition, 6 volt lighting

DIMENSIONS

Wheelbase	51in
Seat height	30in
Overall width	27in
Ground clearance	5in
Kerb weight	296lb
Fuel capacity	3gal
Tyres (original fittings)	
(front)	18 x 3.25 Dunlop
(rear)	16 x 3.25 Dunlop
Brakes	
(front)	6 x 1.1/8in drum
(rear)	6 x 1.1/8in drum

PERFORMANCE

Top speed	78mph (approx.)
Standing ¼ mile	19.5sec (approx.)
Fuel consumption	
(overall)	50mpg
(ridden hard)	45mpg
Braking distance	
(from 30 mph)	41ft
(from 60 mph)	129ft
Owner	John Stretton, Eastbourne

500cc Ariel Red Hunter

by Royce Creasey

Ariel Red Hunter

This is the sort of bike test that journalists everywhere find difficulty with. It's easy to enthuse about the edge experience of riding some barely legal, race-bred rocketship, in fact to enjoy any machine which excels at excess. But most bikes produced in the world are simply motorcycles, and the Ariel Red Hunter is a remarkably representative example of such a machine. While Velocette and Norton, and later BSA, were attempting to find out just how thrilling a single-cylinder bike could be, and Royal Enfield were discovering how much torque such a device could produce, Ariel concentrated on Making Motorcycles. Reading through the history of the marque gives a clue; time and time again I'd come across reference to the determination of the company to obtain reliability, to anticipate market needs. It's only 25 years later, when you see the surviving result, that it's apparent that they succeeded; the Red Hunter is a classic example of a machine that's quick enough to keep you awake and yet soft enough to avoid injuring you.

Technically, the Red Hunter is quite an interesting design. In the mid-fifties bikes were going through a generation change. The old bicycle frames were giving way to the modern bicycle frames which at least had suspension at both ends, and commonly attempted to give the plot some degree of stiffness. Engines had reached the point where they generally did what was required, and a process of 'tidying-up' was widespread. Lights had at least become part of the package, although this implied nothing impressive in terms of output or reliability. All these influences are visible in the Red Hunter. The frame, in 1955, was bang up-to-date, being a full duplex cradle with swinging-arm rear suspension. The swinging-arm itself is unique in being fabricated from pressed steel rather than tubing, a constructional method eventually used by this company for the later two-strokes. Its use for an otherwise conventional swinging-arm is rather less practical, but this frame at least picked up the swinging-arm pivots at the outer ends, unlike Velocette and Triumph who both persevered with the old 'universal joint' method for another ten years. The front forks are remarkably similar in appearance and operation to the contemporary BSA units, but I am assured that they are in fact Ariel through and through. It's probable, however, as

Not the quickest, or most torquey, Ariel's Red Hunter is a bike for all seasons – a reliable all rounder.

497cc engine features cast-in pushrod tubes, three main bearings and double row roller big-end.

Clutch runs dry, separated from the oil bath by a vital seal. The MagDyno dates the overall design.

BSA owned Ariel at that time, that some design interchange took place even if manufacture was separate.

Unfortunately, it cannot be said that these cycle parts work particularly well. I rode the bike for four days, but was unable to decide exactly what was wrong with the suspension. Both ends seemed quite softly sprung, and there was no doubt that damping was present in suitable quantities. But the bike just didn't like bumps. It seemed that the suspension couldn't react fast enough, which is usually a sign of excessive unsprung weight. In the Red Hunter's case, however, unsprung weight would appear to be quite low, as the hubs and wheels are quite conventional and in fact relatively clean compared with many bikes of that era. Also, the handling is somewhat strange. The steering 'falls in' just like a modern Japanese bike, and is similarly very light. Happily, there is no trace of instability, no suggestion of weaving or wheel shimmy. Serious mania in terms of cornering is prevented by the centre stand which scrapes safely but loudly at a very moderate rate of lean, but in the area that is available it's noticeable that the bike doesn't sweep through turns in the way expected of English machinery. It has to be steered, and one comes to the conclusion that Ariel steering geometry could have been better, at least on this frame.

The engine is similarly up to date by the standards of the mid-fifties. Based on a much older design, started in 1934 (another period of generation change) and with a bottom end identical to its predecessors and its side-valve kin, the main changes were intended to produce a 'cleaner running' unit. Thus the pushrod tubes, a source of oil leaks on every bike that uses them, are cast into the barrel. The top end of the engine is generally very tidy, and in fact compared to the bottom end looks much more modern. Perhaps it's just that the mag-dyno unit dates it.

In line with Ariel's attempts to produce a reliable, popular bike, the engine is completely unexcessive in characteristics. It ticks over and picks up well, but not exceptionally. It propels this quite heavy bike fast enough, but not especially fast. There is no real power band, no sensitive response to the throttle. But at the same time it avoids the problems with snatch and 'flat spots' often encountered with its hairier contemporaries. On the road the Red Hunter trucks along between 50 and 70mph without fuss, getting progressively buzzier as 70 is passed and sounding best at

The six volt Cibié headlight is a new addition to the otherwise standard machine.

around 60. The moderate power output and quite low torque figure mean that higher speeds than the legal limit are unlikely to be reached very often, it's just too much effort. At first the motor feels like a much earlier unit in a low state of tune, and possibly fragile, but the realisation comes that it is probably unbreakable, that it is a relatively modern engine in a low state of tune, and thus unlikely to be overloaded.

Looking at the bike's technical specification confirms this impression. Mains and big-end are right up-to-date for the mid-fifties, and compare favourably with Velocette's arrangements. The crank runs in two ball and one roller bearings, and the big-end is a two-row roller. Lubrication is limited by the touch of Mr Turner, whose plunger pump pushes the oil around, but this device manages to keep Triumphs oiled and is clearly capable of dealing with the moderate loads encountered in this engine. The oil used in this bike is the excellent Silkolene Chatsworth straight-40. Transmission damping is taken care of by a conventional face-cam crankshaft shock absorber, but convention stops at the clutch. This component differs radically from mid-fifties' practice by running dry. The clutch chain-wheel is a separate wheel, running through a seal on its shaft to the clutch which is housed separately. The friction material is cork, which is quite happy to work dry, as long as it doesn't get oily. It's clear that oil seal problems would lead to a slipping clutch, but this does not appear to happen. I don't see any major advantages in running a clutch dry like this, but it should be noted that the result in this case is very pleasant. Unusually, for a bike from this era, the clutch can take being held in while the machine is at a standstill for prolonged periods

Forks look similar to BSA units, but were made at Selly Oak. Front brake is not up to modern conditions.

Top lever on the unusual dual control is a decompressor, the other controls magneto advance and retard.

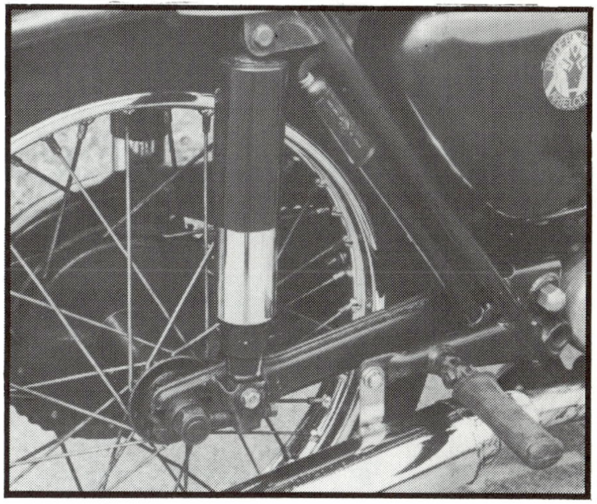

Tidy at the back end, the Red Hunter features a pressed steel swinging arm and Blumell's cycle pump.

without any distress. Neutral can be selected at a standstill without difficulty, and the action is light and progressive.

The gearbox is remarkable. It's undoubtedly the slowest change in the whole world. Even the Reliant box used in that futuristic phenomenon the Quasar, with its full synchromesh and the holder of the 'world's slowest' title until now, is substantially faster. But once the correct timing has been achieved it's possible to make clean, silent changes with this Burman unit. It's just that the timing is similar to that used in Presenting Arms at Slow March. Once again, the gearbox is a part of the bike you will not be able to break.

Lighting is provided by the almost universal Lucas dynamo/regulator set-up, the dynamo, as mentioned before, being part of the mag-dyno unit. The test bike was fitted with the six-volt Cibie conversion which will melt a Miller dynamo, but forms an excellent working relationship with the Lucas unit. The regulator is located directly on the frame and, as is usual when such a component is subjected to the vibration from a single-cylinder engine, is a little erratic in output. The battery is mounted in the old way, with a strap, despite the adoption of neat and matching boxes for the oil and tools. This could be expected to cause a short and unreliable life on a faster bike, but watching it work it's clear that it's all OK on the Ariel.

In evaluating the overall effect a bike has I find that it's often impossible to make an objective decision. One has to watch one's feelings instead. Having ridden the Red Hunter long enough to have adjusted to its pace I found that I enjoyed it. The pace I found nicest was sufficiently relaxed to allow me some appreciation of the view, the countryside and my errant daydreams. At the same time the bike covered the ground quickly enough to prevent boredom setting in. I'd try and avoid riding 300 miles in a winter

Handling is safe without being exceptional. The steering tends to 'fall in' but doesn't shimmy.

rainstorm on it, but I'd also turn down that opportunity on anything lacking weather protection. For "streaking down country lanes" as Ariel put it, it's really rather nice in a deliberate, unhurriable sort of way. For its chosen purpose today, taking owner Jeff Thomason to and from work, its complete reliability, coupled with the low-stress pace, is ideal. Several modern bikes approach things in the same way, notably MZ, but compared with these products the Ariel looks much more convincing and makes a far nicer noise.

The only point I found seriously adrift in modern traffic was the braking performance. Both front and rear brakes are smooth and progressive, but they belong to another age; they simply don't possess the ability to pull the emergency stops that are sometimes required in commuter traffic. Of course it's quite reasonable to point out that an emergency stop is the end result of poor riding, and I agree. It's just that I occasionally realise that I'm riding poorly, and such an occasion is quite likely to crop up when going to work or coming home. I've come across this sort of braking performance before on bikes of similar age, and it's hardly the fault of the machines that traffic densities have increased so heavily in the last 15 or 20 years. After all, said densities will soon drop dramatically, and so perhaps the Red Hunter's brakes will prove to be just right after all.

Jeff Thomason is the Ariel Owners' club's technical expert. He's been using the bike since 1975 when he bought it as a complete machine from a breaker. Since then he's been running it to work and back, averaging 7,000 miles a year. There's been virtually no trouble, just the usual persistent oil leaks, the odd problem with lights and other peripherals, and at the time of the test a deafening backfire which usually occurred in the middle of small towns and villages. It's clear that as a working bike Jeff's Red Hunter is well ahead of my Venom on running costs, while turning in a similar fuel consumption figure of around 60mpg. It scores again, however, by being content with two-star. By and large it probably compares quite well with the Royal Enfield Bullet in the role of a working machine that earns its keep.

Starting is really easy. This is not one of those singles that requires any sort of procedure before it'll condescend to fire up. The top lever on the novel twin-lever control is a decompressor, and once the motor has been pushed past compression it's simply a matter of heaving the pedal down. The owners' club is a well-organised outfit with separate sections for the two-strokes, the four-strokes and the Square Fours, and original spares are still obtainable in reasonable quantities. When that source dries up, the club should be able to ensure a supply of more expensive but high-quality replacements. This is the sort of bike that will still be taking someone to work or on holiday, long after loonies like me have worn out the last Velocette.

Specification

500cc ARIEL RED HUNTER

ENGINE

Type	ohv single
Bore x stroke	81.5 x 95mm
Capacity	497cc
Compression ratio	6.8:1
Carburation	Amal 376
Bhp @ rpm	26 @ 6,000
Primary drive	single-row chain
Clutch	multi-plate, dry
Gearbox	4 speed
Electrical system	Lucas 6v 56w dynamo and AVC

DIMENSIONS

Wheelbase	56in
Seat height	31in
Ground clearance	5.5in
Kerb weight	404lb
Fuel capacity	4gal
Tyres	
(front)	3.25 x 19in Avon
(rear)	3.50 x 19in Dunlop
Brakes	
(front)	7in sls
(rear)	7in sls

PERFORMANCE

Top speed	80-85mph (catalogue figure)
Standing ¼ mile	18 sec (est)
Fuel consumption	60mpg
Braking distance from 30mph	29ft
Owner	Jeff Thomason, Luton, Beds.

997cc Ariel Square Four

by Royce Creasey

Ariel Square Four

It would be all too easy to dismiss the Ariel Square Four as yet another of those brilliant English inventions that doesn't actually, er . . . work. Indeed, certain components on the machine undoubtedly fall into that category. In practice, however, the Square Four is saved from such a summary dismissal by the considerable promise shown by its unusual engine layout. Bear in mind that one of today's fastest Grand Prix machines uses the same arrangement of cylinders, albeit with the essential addition of water cooling and the rather more dubious advantage of two-stroke operation.

The test bike is one of the first Mk II Square Fours, and its year of origin, 1953, was a period of transition from the Mk I. Thus the front mudguard is the deeply valanced earlier type, the headlight is uncowled, and, more important, the bike lacks the SU carburettor and the different frame required to accommodate it that did not appear until 1954.

Keen students will note that due to the difficulty of attaching cellulose paint to chrome, the rear rim is unpainted. I am assured however, that the paint colour is quite authentic for this year. The Square Four engine suffered from overheating from its inception, and a further modification for the '54 Mk II was an oil tank stretched to a capacity of one gallon from this version's $6\frac{1}{2}$ pints. Apparently the majority of the '53 Mk Is went to Australian and New Zealand police forces, and the model is quite rare in this country.

The engine is very much what this bike is all about, and the unit has an eventful development history. At its inception the Square Four was an extremely advanced design. Laid out originally with an integral gearbox, it was based on two 180-degree parallel twins, with overhung cranks and central gear coupling. Valve gear was operated by a chain-driven overhead camshaft, with drive being taken from the centre of the rear crank. Production difficulties and the need to use a gearbox from the rest of the Ariel range diluted the concept somewhat, but in 1931 the resulting 500 was a radically compact and revvy unit.

The project belongs to the same E. Turner who

A transitional model, this Mk II still has the mudguard, headlight and Solex carb of the Mk I.

The steering damper is a useful item, as the suspension gives rise to some peculiar ride characteristics.

Square Fours were always prone to overheating but alloy castings and a four pipe head improved matters slightly.

gave the world the parallel twin and the plunger oil pump, and initial response was clearly good enough for the firm to bring out a 600cc unit the following year. But two basic flaws dogged the design throughout its production life. The original engine was all cast iron and this, coupled with its compactness, resulted in major overheating problems. In addition, the cylinder head fixing was inadequate. Although the engine clearly had considerable potential for high performance work, early tuning attempts, including the use of supercharging, invariably resulted in gasket troubles. In '34 the Ariel range was standardised around one frame, and the sump and crankcase of the Square Four was redesigned to improve lubrication.

Probably as a result of these problems the major market for the machine was as a sidecar bike, where its smooth power and excellent low-speed response proved most useful. However, in 1936 there came another redesign in what looks like an attempt to reduce the overheating. Pushrods now operated the valves, and capacities of 600 and 1,000cc were offered. In effect, the engine was 'spread out' a bit, and of course the bigger unit could be expected to have an easier time.

These modifications appear to have taken care of gasket blowing, but other problems emerged. Seizure of the rear cylinders may be a largely mythical defect, but failure of the rear rods was not uncommon and may have been caused by lubrication inadequacies at the big-ends. At higher revs, problems with camshaft whip also occurred.

After the war Ariel made another attempt to sort out the engine and came up with the all-alloy Mk I. The centre coupling gears moved to the drive side and the cranks became conventional. Plain bearings were adopted for the big-ends, pushrod operation was retained, and the Mk I engine is visually similar to the Mk II except for its twin exhausts. Although fatter than the pre-war engine the Mk I was, and is, a very small one-litre unit. The change to aluminium from cast iron is said to have saved considerable weight and improved the handling.

But the overheating persisted, possibly as a result of road improvements during those years that permitted higher speeds, and Mk II is the result of still further modification. The four-pipe arrangement is an attempt to pass air over the exhaust ports, and effected some improvement. But camshaft whip, the occasional rod failure and serious overheating persisted, yet the model was not developed after 1954 except for the construction of a prototype with swinging-arm Hunter frame at the very end of Ariel's existence.

Ariel Square Four

The full strangeness of the Square Four is revealed when you examine its frame. The motor has the potential and feel of a Honda four, but the frame definitely belongs to the pre-war era. While Norton had the Featherbed, Velocette offered accurate adjustment of the rear units and Vincent used hydraulic damping at both ends, Ariel relied on the Anstey link. The principal function of this device is to combine constant chain tension with suspension movement. The degree of movement is strictly limited, but considering the total lack of damping at the rear end, this is no bad thing.

Rapid wear is another feature of the Square Four's rear-end layout — the units on the test bike had worn right through their bushes before the rebuild. The lack of damping and the inherent absence of stiffness in the new linkages on the machine produced a more or less continuous Dutch roll at the rear, and gave the same sort of directional stability as a punt would enjoy from the addition of an outboard motor.

This rear suspension system was fitted to all the Square Fours and is another reason for the machine's popularity as a sidecar hauler. And as if to clinch the matter, the front suspension, although reasonably stiff for early telescopics, is also undamped. That is, Ariel claim it is damped, but study of the design reveals only hydraulic stops and the fork is effectively identical to the BSA unit. In operation it certainly behaves in an undamped fashion — recovery from braking plunge at a standstill is rapid enough to lift the front wheel! When under way the front end interacts more or less continually with the oscillations from the rear, and at times the sensation is uncannily like riding a horse. A further handling peculiarity is the low-frequency wheel patter that follows the braking dive onto the bump stops.

All this uncontrolled springing is alleviated by steering geometry which would be quite suitable at three-figure speeds, a stiff frame, and a very low centre of gravity. Due to the latter, rapid directional changes can be made, and once the suspension has been allowed for it's easy to ride the bike quite quickly. The performance and suspension combine most usefully in traffic, where the Square Four resembles an ultra-light Norton Commando in the way it can be dropped into a gap on the steering and wound out on the throttle. Catch it right and the suspension bounce will provide further assistance.

Another aid to urban riding is the dry clutch similar to that fitted on the Red Hunter. Unlike its contemporaries, this unit allows the rider to hold the bike in gear at a standstill, or to find neutral easily. It appears unaffected by heat and is pleasingly light.

Unfortunately, traffic use brings on the infamous Square Four overheating problem, and this is exaggerated by the Solex carburettor which, on the test bike at least, suffered from a flat spot and what appeared to be fuel boiling. The engine tended to mis-

The ingenious swinging link rear suspension gives limited wheel movement and wears bushes rapidly.

Like the Red Hunter, the clutch ran dry. A good unit, it makes riding in heavy traffic light work.

A car-type distributor feeds the spark plugs of the remarkably compact, smooth and torquey motor.

fire after fairly short periods in town, and went through a period of cutting out completely. I was very relieved to note that there was no sign of seizure or loss of compression after this session.

Out of town the bike was finally able to settle into a relaxed state. Apart from a vibration period at just over 60mph it is a very smooth motorcycle. The factory quoted a maximum speed of 105mph for this model, and I got close to that figure with the engine showing no signs of distress. Once past its vibration area the big Ariel feels increasingly like a very smooth modern motorcycle engine. Noise levels at lower speeds are similar to a Triumph Thunderbird and indeed, that is the bike the Square Four most resembles — minus the vibration.

My main objection to the machine's high-speed response rests with the suspension — horses lack stability at speed! Perhaps the best suggestion for the Square Four's ideal use comes from Ariel's description of the Red Hunter. The Hunter, said the factory, was for streaking down country lanes. But unlike the Hunter, the Square Four really does streak, the brakes work, and at 50-60mph the low centre of gravity and reasonable weight compensate for the lack of damping.

In the absence of motorways and modern "A" roads the bike would clearly make a quiet and smooth tourer, with a degree of initial acceleration superior to any of the sporting singles of its day. It runs convincingly on two-star fuel and has a five-gallon tank. Consumption worked out at around 47mpg, but I'm sure this would be improved by a better carburettor.

A secondary advantage of the lack of vibration is that the electrics, although quite conventional for the period, seem reliable. There is a larger dynamo and a big battery, presumably with sidecar use in mind, but even so a steady ammeter needle at 50mph is a rare sight on any English motorcycle. I was also impressed to note that despite all the moving parts in the engine, oil consumption was effectively nil. The motor is fairly new, having been recently rebuilt by Healey Engineering, and it is probable that use will

Not the world's best bend swinger, the Squariel became a popular machine for sidecar duties.

loosen it up somewhat — the improvement in performance and general feel after 15 or 20 miles of open-road riding was quite noticeable. Overheating does seem to be a problem confined to town use, although it is probable that short journeys might result in condensation in the crankcase even though the heads are cooking.

It may at first seem odd that such a promising design should go through a production life of nearly 30 years without such basic defects in engine design and suspension operation going unrectified. Allowance has to be made for the Second World War, but possibly more pertinent to this neglect is that Ariel seemed to be in a continual process of corporate reorganisation. The company's owner during the inception of the Square Four was Jack Sangster, and chief designers and engineers included Val Page, Edward Turner and Bert Hopwood. During the war Sangster sold his interest to BSA, under various conditions, and the design staff went on to Triumph and BSA. Several innovative projects developed by Ariel were killed by BSA, and there is evidence of plenty of corporate interference in development programmes. Even so, it's hard to escape the impression that Ariel only produced modifications to the Square Four in order to solve problems with existing models. A more farsighted approach could have turned the Square Four into a very modern motorcycle.

The Healey organisation, which rebuilt the engine of the test bike, certainly held this view and during the late sixties and early seventies produced the Healey Four to special order. The pre-war cycle was replaced by an Egli unit, and this modification presumably disposed of all the Square Four handling problems. The motor was essentially the Mk II, but extensive work was done to the lubrication system and the heads were reworked. The lack of suitable engines for conversion unfortunately ended this interesting project, and I've never seen a Healey let alone ridden this rare bike.

As Ariel sold it, the Square Four clearly failed to exploit its advantages of a low centre of gravity, compactness and lack of vibration. Water cooling would seem to be essential for this layout, and although very pleasant in the right conditions, with an unbeatable lack of vibration, the machine suffers by comparison with other big touring bikes of the day. It seems unfair to compare the Square Four with the Vincent, but this is the bike it would have competed with in the market. The Vincent offers a level of performance which relates to a modern one-litre motorcycle, but the Square Four most definitely does not. Its innovative engine assures it of a place in history, but as a road-going motorcycle it has to be classed not as one of the great machines, but as one that could have been great if only . . .

Specification

1953 ARIEL SQUARE FOUR Mk II

ENGINE

Type	ohv square four
Bore x stroke	65 x 75mm
Capacity	997cc
Compression ratio	7.2:1
Carburation	Solex
Bhp @ rpm	40 @ 5,600
Electrical	70w 6v Lucas dynamo/regulator; 20 amp-hour battery; coil and distributor ignition
Primary drive	single-row chain
Clutch	multi-plate, dry
Gearbox	4 speed

DIMENSIONS

Frame	tubular
Suspension	
(front)	telescopic
(rear)	Anstey link, combined undamped plunger and rocker system
Wheels	
(front)	3.25 x 19
(rear)	4.00 x 19
Brakes	
(front)	7in sls drum
(rear)	7in sls drum
Wheelbase	56½in
Seat height	30in
Ground clearance	5½in
Dry weight	460lb
Fuel capacity	5gal

PERFORMANCE

Top speed	105mph (est)
Standing ¼ mile	15.5secs (est)
Fuel consumption	47mpg
Owner	Ray Kilham, London

500cc DBD34 BSA Gold Star Clubman and Roadster

Royce Creasey

BSA Gold Star

The elegant good looks of the DBD34 Gold Stars on test undoubtedly account for a considerable part of this design's popularity. The compact tidiness of the whole machine compares favourably with any modern bike and was exceptional in the latter half of the fifties.

But this does not explain the myth that surrounds these BSAs. More than any other machine I've owned or tested, the legend of the Goldie has survived the passage of the last twenty-odd years. Even modern Yamaha advertising seems aware of the tradition, although the Yamaha concerned is more closely related to the Honda 50.

It happens that I had always been unaware of the reasons for this reverence. Previous contact with this model in the 'rocker' days wasn't encouraging, being confined mainly to helping with push starts and plug changes at traffic lights. One heard various rumours, of course, concerning ridiculous speeds in first gear, and it must be admitted that any cafe-racer worthy of the name had to be geared up until a satisfactory clutch-slipping start could be obtained.

Shortly after setting off on the test Clubman, the reason for the myth became apparent. Try and imagine Honda offering a street-legal version of their one-litre RCB endurance racer, reasonably priced and backed by the normal guarantee. Silencing and other details would be present but strictly limited so as not to impair performance, which would be up to full-house, track-tune standards. The machine would be set up for the TT circuit.

You can appreciate that after six or seven years of production and the sale of well over 20,000 bikes to all and sundry there would be a public outcry, a dedicated legion of worshippers, and commercial copiers everywhere. This would, of course, result in the condemnation of anything that even looked similar by all right-thinking people. Thus it was with the Gold Star. The entire cafe-racer tradition can be laid at the wheels of this motorcycle.

Take the simple matter of slow-moving traffic. Gearing on the Clubman is such that clutch slip is necessary in bottom gear up to around the legal limit for urban streets if the engine is to remain above 3,000rpm. The engine produces no power below this point and stops working below about 2,000rpm. In addition to this trick, the Amal GP carb is a pure racing instrument. Below a 75 per cent throttle opening it's just a tube with petrol pouring down it, and this petrol wets the plug unless the motor is run up to around

Fork-top layout of the Clubman is in classic cafe racer style, as is the quick release petrol cap.

One of the best known power units of all time, the almost 'square' 500cc single gave up to 42bhp.

Crude by modern standards the Amal GP carb made starting and riding at low speeds a test of skill.

5,000rpm occasionally — say every thirty seconds in traffic.

The silencer appears to exist primarily to produce the famous, and quite attractive 'twitter'. Just keeping the engine running in town, and keeping up with traffic stops conversation, rattles windows and makes cyclists forget to pedal. It's not an irritating noise, it's paralysing. More throttle makes more noise and full throttle at speed makes thinking impossible. It's difficult to avoid the impression that some part of the bike has caught on the road surface and is tearing it down the dotted line.

The Clubman riding position suits the motor well. This, and the tendency to top heaviness, makes slow-speed work difficult, but the seat height is low enough at 30½in for even my legs to make it to the ground. All this may sound outrageous for road use, and it really is. As a racer, however, the Clubman's Goldie is about average at low speed and any consideration of the qualities of this bike has to be limited to the other end of the speed range. The TT is a fast circuit and consequently a good A road is necessary to get a Clubman moving.

At speed it really is good. The motor is probably the strongest 500cc production single yet made. Authoritative sources quote 42-43bhp as the highest figure the unit produced, while the factory test sheet for the Roadster tested gave 37.2bhp at 7,000rpm. Torque on that engine was listed as a useful 30ft-lbs at 5,500rpm, similar to the modern Yamaha in engine speed at least. As would be expected, this urge is most noticeable at full throttle and high revs. The increase in power over the last thousand rpm is very obvious, and the very close-ratio box has to be used hard to keep the engine in that range. There are multis that accelerate faster, but of the singles I've ridden only the 450 desmo Ducati comes near to the feeling of the Gold Star gathering speed at full bore.

The cycle parts keep up with all this surprisingly well. Apart from a kink in a frame tube to clear the oil pump, everything is B31, that less-than-devastating but useful hack. A later, and common, modification to the Clubman is the two-way damped forks, identified by the extra nuts in the stanchion-retaining nuts. At speed it rapidly becomes clear that damping is the major weakness of the cycle. The frame and forks are stiff enough, similar in fact to a late, fully-braced Royal Enfield. Steering is on the quick side of the classic compromise used by Vincent, Velocette and Ducati, but very acceptable and quite appropriate for a racing motorcycle. The top-heavy feel makes direction changes something of an effort, but stability is fine; once a line has been confirmed lots of power can be applied, and balanced by body movement, without upsetting the bike.

But the wheels won't stay on the ground. On

several occasions through a series of corners the bike seemed to get into a sort of 'galloping along' state where there was always one wheel off the ground, and often both. Nothing got out of shape during these antics, but of course they make steering and power changes somewhat difficult. After an afternoon of posing for the camera at less than racing speeds on a reasonable A road, I have to conclude that I have considerable respect for the people who raced these bikes, and won almost every time, on the TT circuit of the early fifties. They most definitely had something I haven't got, and even if it was only bone and muscle the difference is substantial. It's necessary to ride a Goldie 'short stirrup', taking the weight on the hands and feet to avoid the bucking seat, and after this fairly short test my legs ached for days.

Given the ancestry of the cycle parts it's clear that the engine is the sole reason for all this drama. Accepting its pure racing breeding, the output from this pushrod single is still extraordinary. My main research task was to discover the reason for figures which Velocette (for instance), with a far better pedigree in racing, could not match. A look inside the Gold Star's head sufficed. Instead of the pair of dinner plates commonly found acting as valves in contemporary 'high performance' engines, the Goldie units look Ducati-sized. This is a small-valve motor, the ports taper the right way, and the size differential between the inlet and exhaust is distinctly modern.

This is a satisfactory reason for the performance, but raises the question of how BSA discovered that which eluded so many others. It turns out to be another of those happy accidents on which the English motorcycle industry seemed to survive. Gold Star production was strictly limited to what was available in the way of tooling, major components and what sold best. When the post-war design was being defined the biggest market, even for the Goldie, was for trials work. The small-valve head was therefore chosen, and due to BSA's habit of doing development work on the dyno, later experiments revealed that bigger valves didn't work any better. Development was instead concentrated on port shapes and angles, and the inevitable stiffening and strengthening

The Goldie was first and foremost a racing machine – and even wearing road trim it looks like one.

required to cope with the steady increase in power. The development history of the Gold Star is in fact a classic story of rational research and careful improvement, not least because it seems to have been a rare process in post-war England!

Two things conspired to prevent this effort resulting in a really fine road bike. First, all the work was aimed at producing a good race bike, and with outstanding success. Today racing is the endless sound of Yamahas; in the early fifties it was the endless sound of Goldies. More serious was the BSA policy directive that all tooling and patterns had to be based on the main production of B31 and B33 singles. This eventually resulted in the situation where the Goldie was a modern bike in prototype form limited only by its increasingly obsolete production origins.

When the production range changed, concentrating on the twins, the Goldie had to stop. Without the supply of cheap parts, high assembly and testing costs, caused largely by the primitive nature of those parts, rendered production unviable. Velocette ran into the same difficulties with the Thruxton Venom some years later, and for the same reasons. The Ducati single can be seen as a Gold Star engine made with modern tools and materials and is perhaps a nicer unit than the C15.

The major weakness of the Goldie engine is reputedly the crankshaft. Although based on the production components, it went through various changes in size, shape and material. It's a 'built-up' unit, as was common to singles of that period, and development concentrated on increasing its stiffness as much as possible. Although the collection of pressings, nuts, taper fits and rivets can reasonably cause raised engineering eyebrows, the unit in detail does appear to have considerable rigidity. The big-end is a massively lubricated two-row roller, and the mains are an imposing collection of large ball and roller bearings.

By comparison, the admittedly rather narrower Velo unit looks hopelessly inadequate, and I tend to the conclusion that at Gold Star outputs and speeds, built-up cranks are marginal regardless of how they are done. Significantly, the development team did try for a one-piece crank with a plain big end, which is where the extra oil came from, but for reasons possibly connected with the aforementioned policy directive it was not used in production.

The remainder of the power train is conventional BSA, apart from the Clubman's RRT2 close-ratio box which has needle-roller tail bearings, but usefully retains the kickstart. This is all well known equipment with a reputation for strength, and even the demands of the Clubman power unit didn't worry it. The clutch might lose an inch of adjustment in town, but it always came back eventually and the gearchange was typically light and easy. This package is not especially smooth, certainly not as a Royal Enfield is smooth, but given the designated operating conditions this is of little importance.

Front brake is adequate, while the undamped forks provide safe but exhilarating handling.

Such elegance of design makes the Goldie the definitive sports machine of its era – of any era come to that.

It is to BSA's credit that they did try to present the Goldie in a more reasonable form. The Roadster tested was the result. Apart from the forward footrests and conventional bars (Vincent bars are fitted to this bike), which make the machine much easier to ride at low speed, the gearbox has normally-spaced ratios and road gearing. The engine is a mildly detuned version of the Clubman — and the accent is on 'mildly'. Compression ratio is lower and the cams are a different pair from the large range available. Most useful change is the big Concentric, and while the motor is still extremely dubious about running clean below 2,000rpm, it does run. With care it's possible to pretend that it's just a B31 chuffing through traffic; the ignition retard helps this effect.

All pretence vanishes as soon as the throttle is

opened, however. The silencing arrangements are identical to the Clubman's, and the motor is just as enthusiastic about running straight round to seven grand. As a late-night street racer the tourer showed devastating form, principally because the noise overwhelmed any opposition. Naturally every policeman I passed seemed to think World War Three had just stated, and I suddenly rejected plans to visit the old north London rocker haunts on the grounds of possible environmental damage, mainly to my licence.

Instead I terrorised various small villages on the outskirts, just as it was done in the old days. On such roads the Roadster really comes into its own. The gearing is a little low for modern highways, but ideal for the backroads. The motor, which buzzes when cruising, is perfect for constant acceleration. The brakes are, er... useful, and the handling is safe but very exciting. The standard forks set a tradition in cafe racing so faithfully followed by the Enfield Continental GT tested recently, and are undamped. The flat bars and simplistic front suspension produce a degree of front wheel lifting which is less noticeable on the Clubman and suggests that the Roadster's centre of gravity is slightly too far back.

From the rider's point of view this package is very good indeed. The level of excitement and physical activity are high enough to burn out pleasure centres for a week, leading naturally to weekly doses, and the

Where the wild things are . . . BSA's Gold Star demands to be ridden hard and fast, and amply rewards the rider.

erection of barricades by local villagers. Maybe I've got an overdeveloped social conscience, but I'd have trouble justifying the pleasure I got out of riding the bike to all the people who were stunned by the noise.

When it comes to consideration of social uses of the Gold Star, it displays its talents best when parked. I went to have a look at the old Cellar cafe in Windsor. Naturally the place is now just a hole in the ground (was it ever more?) but there's a nice pub just down the road and I parked the Roadster there while I had lunch. Sitting outside, looking across the river, it's very easy to blur out all the modern cars and just see the real things like the river banks, the old bridge, the ducks — and the Gold Star — in focus. It sure looked good to me, and I soon found out that it looked good to other people, too. It turns out that if you talk to most blokes in their late thirties they either had, wanted, or still want a Gold Star. Standing around the pub door with several such randomly-met people, most of whom knew more about Goldies than I did, it was easy to see back to the days when that road had been full of bikes just like this one. When bikes really were incredibly noisy, dangerously fast — and totally anti-social. But the Gold Star looked just right parked and a surprising amount of people are happy just to stand and look at one.

Peter Richardson, the owner of both the test bikes and a Rocket Gold Star which he personally prefers, is quite ready to admit that he rarely rides either Goldie far. This is a criticism often levelled at collectors by users, but in the case of the Gold Star it would be unreasonable to ask anyone to ride one all the time. There is a limit to the excitement and effort that the human frame can take, and any racing bike on the road will be well beyond this limit. The Goldie takes it all too far with a splendid lack of compromise and a style which defined the term 'fast motorcycle' for over a decade.

it is virtually impossible to relate this bike to any of the other road-going 500cc singles of its day. The Venom/Thruxton pair are the most obvious candidates for comparison, and of course I was in the position of stepping off one and onto the other — in the shape of my own Venom — in the course of the test. In fact the two machines achieve their respective qualities in such different ways that comparison is of limited use. It could obviously be said that the Goldie motor is much more powerful and much less flexible than a Venom unit, that the Velo cycle is much more confortable, but much more flexible, but this would be true of any racer-roadster comparison.

If I were to race one of the two it would be the Goldie; if I were to ride one on the road it would be the Velo. If I could only sit and look, then again the choice would be the Goldie. It's easier to identify its prime quality. As the Velocette is awarded Most Useful Accident, and the Vincent gets Most...!, the Goldie unquestionably qualifies for Most Outrageous.

Specification

1960 BSA GOLD STAR DBD34 CLUBMAN & ROADSTER

(Figures for Roadster, where different, are in brackets.)

ENGINE

Type	ohv single
Bore x stroke	85 x 88mm
Capacity	499cc
Compression ratio	9.0:1 (n/a)
Carburation	1½in Amal GP2 (Amal Concentric)
Bhp @ rpm	n/a (37.2 @ 7,000)
Ignition	Lucas Magdyno
Primary drive	single-row chain
Clutch	multi-plate, wet
Gearbox	4 speed

DIMENSIONS

Frame	duplex cradle
Suspension	
(front)	Taylor-Dow two-way damped BSA telescopic front forks (standard undamped BSA telescopics)
(rear)	Girling oil struts
Tyres	
(front)	19 x 3.65 Dunlop TT100
(rear)	19 x 4.10 Dunlop TT100
Brakes	
(front)	7.5in sls drum
(rear)	7.0in sls drum
Wheelbase	56.0in
Seat height	30.5in
Ground clearance	5.0in
Dry weight	350lb (approx)
Fuel capacity	4gal

PERFORMANCE

Top speed	110mph (100mph) – est
Standing ¼mile	n/a (14.5secs – est)
Fuel consumption	45-50mpg
Owner	Peter Richardson

BSA 500cc Royal Star and 650cc Lightning

by Peter Watson

BSA Unit Twins

I can't say that I've ever encountered anyone who was too broken up at the demise of BSA's final parallel twins in 1973. By then the two 650s — the twin carb A65L Lightning and single carb A65T Thunderbolt — were, along with the 500 single B50SS 'Gold Star' and A75 Rocket Three, all that remained of what had once been a huge range of solid, everyday motorcycles. It is true that BSA had produced a 750cc version of their unit-construction twin called the A70, and I know of at least one that trundles happily about the Midlands, but they are rare.

This is hardly a case for beery-eyed sadness. Weep for the Rocket Three if you will — and those who have owned one may weep with you — but shed not a tear for the A65 or A70. Like the Triceratops of 63 million years ago they had developed in ways that left them uncomfortably unable to cope with the challenges of the world in which they found themselves. They were hardly killed off in their prime; already market forces in America had ensured that they were dwindling towards extinction.

Which brings us to this road test and a slightly earlier pair of BSA unit twins: a 1967 Lightning and a 1968 A50 Royal Star. On the face of it they hardly look like suitable material until you pause to consider that there are plenty of motorcyclists looking not just for bizarre and exotic rarities to worship in the peace of a lock-up garage, but something a little more mundane and less expensive to use day in, day out. That's when you start looking for low-mileage British parallel twins. Machines with good handling, plenty of low-down urge; motorcycles that are simple to work on and for which spares are still plentiful. If you really can't stomach the thought of turning up for work in a Ford Cortina or on 250 cubic centimetres of whisperised, denatured boredom, here's a viable alternative.

Looking at either an A50 or A65 of this vintage poses a couple of obvious questions. Are they as desirable as BSA's earlier A7 and A10 500 and 600cc vertical twins? Are they as attractive as their Triumph contemporaries? The 100mph 650cc Triumph 6TA for instance, or a nice clean 500 Daytona? You just can't consider them in isolation unless you see the letters BSA light up in red neon every time you close your eyes. And even then, like my friends Bob and Roger — who both used to own fairly late-model A65s — you may opt for the earlier Small Heath product.

"I've just rebuilt the gearbox on my A10," said Bob when I phoned recently. "It's built like a battleship. That's never going to wear out. Just take the selector plate. On the A65 it's a skeletal affair; on the A10 it's a good, solid piece of work made to take years of wear — it'd last a hundred years." Things like that make people desert a 1972

The unit construction motor looks very small, especially in relation to the unfortunate sidepanels.

A little on the spindly side, the front forks are not overtaxed by the sls brake's stopping power.

Basic instrumentation keeps the fork crown tidy and light, but tank trim is a source of rattles.

Thunderbolt 650 for the pleasures of rebuilding a '54 plunger-sprung A10 Golden Flash. Along with other little considerations such as a better riding position, less vibration, poorer lights and handling and nothing like the same acceleration or top-end performance.

Here is the unit twin's great dilemma. Overweight as they are at around 420lb, their 9:1 pistons — originally 7.25:1 when the A50 and A65 were launched in '62 — and fairly low gearing pack quite a punch. Yet at anything over 55mph real finger-numbing vibration comes pounding through the handlebars (rubber mounting came later; those fat grips aren't much help) and your feet tingle, too. The figures on the odometers in the speedo head are shaken into a meaningless blur. Even on a beautifully sweet-running gem of a Royal Star like this one, with a mere 6,500 miles on its cylinders from new, I felt no desire to cruise at anything over 55mph. The sheer physical assault made upon the human frame by the 499cc, 360-degree twin at 70mph makes motorway riding a pointless exercise. I stuck to the back roads, which are more fun anyway, but caught myself thinking that it's not much use paying for performance that you can't comfortably use. A10s are a lot cheaper than A65s just now; physical suffering is not an end in itself.

And yet I was surprised by this ugly side of the A50's otherwise pleasant nature. In the summer of '76 — you remember, those endless weeks of gorgeous motorcycling weather — Roger, Bob and I and several other like-minded persons headed across the Channel and France to Germany for the BSA Owners' Club annual International Rally. On a borrowed '63 A10 Super Rocket (surely one of the best A10 models built, Rocket Gold Stars notwithstanding), I hacked comfortably around France, Germany and bits of Belgium and Luxembourg for a fortnight. The Super Rocket was superbly comfortable — seat height 30in — beautifully soft and tractable, had a totally enclosed rear chain and was a bit lacking in ground clearance when fully laden. I almost fell completely in love with it until, 30 miles from its unfortunate owner's doorstep, the drive side main bearing started to break up.

In fact I was amazed to discover just how much the unit BSA twins owe to their pre-unit ancestors. Because the engine looks so different externally you forget that it's very much the same basic layout inside — a single, rear-mounted camshaft and so on — and that the cycle parts surrounding it changed very little right up to 1970 when the current Meriden twin's oil-bearing chassis arrived from the boffins at BSA-Triumph's Umberslade Hall R & D department. A great idea if your inside leg measurement was 38in, otherwise a bit painful. . .

The 500 A7 of 1946, basically a pre-war engine delayed by that bit of bother from '39 to '45, was not a truly separate engine and gearbox design like the Norton Model 7 Dominator twin. Its gearbox was bolted to the back of the engine's crankcase in semi-unit fashion with a slipper tensioner for the duplex primary chain. One might have assumed that the whole lot would just gently grow together, like the Triumph twin, in the fullness of time. Despite the obvious engineering sanity of unit construction for engine and gearbox few British motorcycles ever came near to matching the beautifully smooth, all-enclosing lines of the A65/A50 Star Twins of '62. Historically, few manufacturers could be bothered to cut and heat-treat their own gears when first someone like Sturmey Archer and then Burman would do it for them, and at a reasonable price. And there can be distinct advantages to a separate gearbox when you want to ring the changes on a basic theme, however much tensioning the primary chain by shunting the 'box around in between a pair of engine plates is to be abhorred.

Yet if the engines looked superb with their egg-shaped crankcases, the rest of the styling on the unit twins was something of a disaster from the outset. Looking at these two machines they hit you in the eye as being visually bulky and heavy. Major culprits are those ridiculously bulbous plastic side panels, which add next to nothing in weight physically, but whose lines are hopelessly cumbersome. Likewise the seat and tank look unrelated. The superb Super Rocket dual-seat, so closely styled on a sprung saddle and pillion pad, looks right and has you sitting low down in the machine. On both A65 and A50 I felt perched on top of the world, despite being only 32 inches off the road and easily able to plant both soles firmly on tarmac. The riding position is poor with those curious curly bars, a hard seat and footrests too far forward. And they didn't extend the saddle when adding that racy hump — passengers usually have to sit on top of it.

From its teles-and-rigid-rear days of 1946 the A7 progressed to plunger springing in '48. The 646cc A10 Golden Flash was launched in 1949 and although externally not greatly changed from the iron-head 500, inside the combustion chambers assumed a more hemispherical shape and the porting was completely rearranged. Bert Hopwood was back from Norton and things were looking up for BSA. A fairly well-supported swinging arm pivoting on phosphor-bronze bushes followed first as an option and then as standard equipment. It's worth noting that this 'extras' policy hung on a long time: 12-volt electrics were extra as late as 1964. As with the majority of post-war designs, the chassis just grew and metamorphosed rather than changing radically. In this case there was little need for it to do so, with such a basically sound semi-double cradle structure. For the unit twins the major change was all-welded construction. The front forks on our Lightning and Royal Star also possess what one road tester of the period described as 'a semblance of two-way damping'. You can convert the A7/10 forks, but they still feel harsh on compression and top out easily on the rebound stroke.

The handling of both machines — which feature almost identical running gear bar a lick of chrome here and there — is really rather good, despite heavily sprung and unyielding Girling units at the rear and the front forks' deficiencies. Closed fork ends on the swinging arm is a nice touch, everything feels nicely stiff and the handling is neutral. A curious mixture of the original Dunlop rib and TT 100 tyres failed to upset the A50, which I soon had pitched hard over into the turns without touching anything down. And as it would pull top gear from as little as 19mph without complaint it was all too tempting to stay in fourth all the time, even for really tight corners, just for the pleasure of hearing the motor *blat-blat-blat* out of a slow turn. This obviously does the transmission no good at all and the intermediate ratios – even on the low mileage 500 — gave off some noise, especially noticeable on the overrun. Surprisingly, the clutch action on both machines was fairly light, unlike the post-1970 engines with their heavier clutch springs and three-ball cam-plate mechanism for the clutch pushrod which develops wrists of iron. I found the gear levers too short for my size tens and soon discovered that the box doesn't like to be rushed any more than an A10's. The lever throw is fairly short, but you can often hear the selector plate clicking away.

Old-fashioned but useful fittings as standard are friction steering dampers — useful for sidecar driving; this A65L used to tow a chair and lugs are provided — and QD rear wheels. Sadly, the A10's optional totally enclosed chaincase, which was carried over on to the ealier unit twins, had disappeared by '67, and the QD wheel can cause real problems. This is because it's a splined type, with the female half of the arrangement attached to the back of the brake drum with six substantial-looking rivets. Not only do the splines wear — like Triumphs of the same period — which causes annoying chattering after a high mileage, but the rivets also have a tendency to find the Lightning's

Right: a weak bottom end mars the unit engine, which shares much in common with its predecessor the A10.

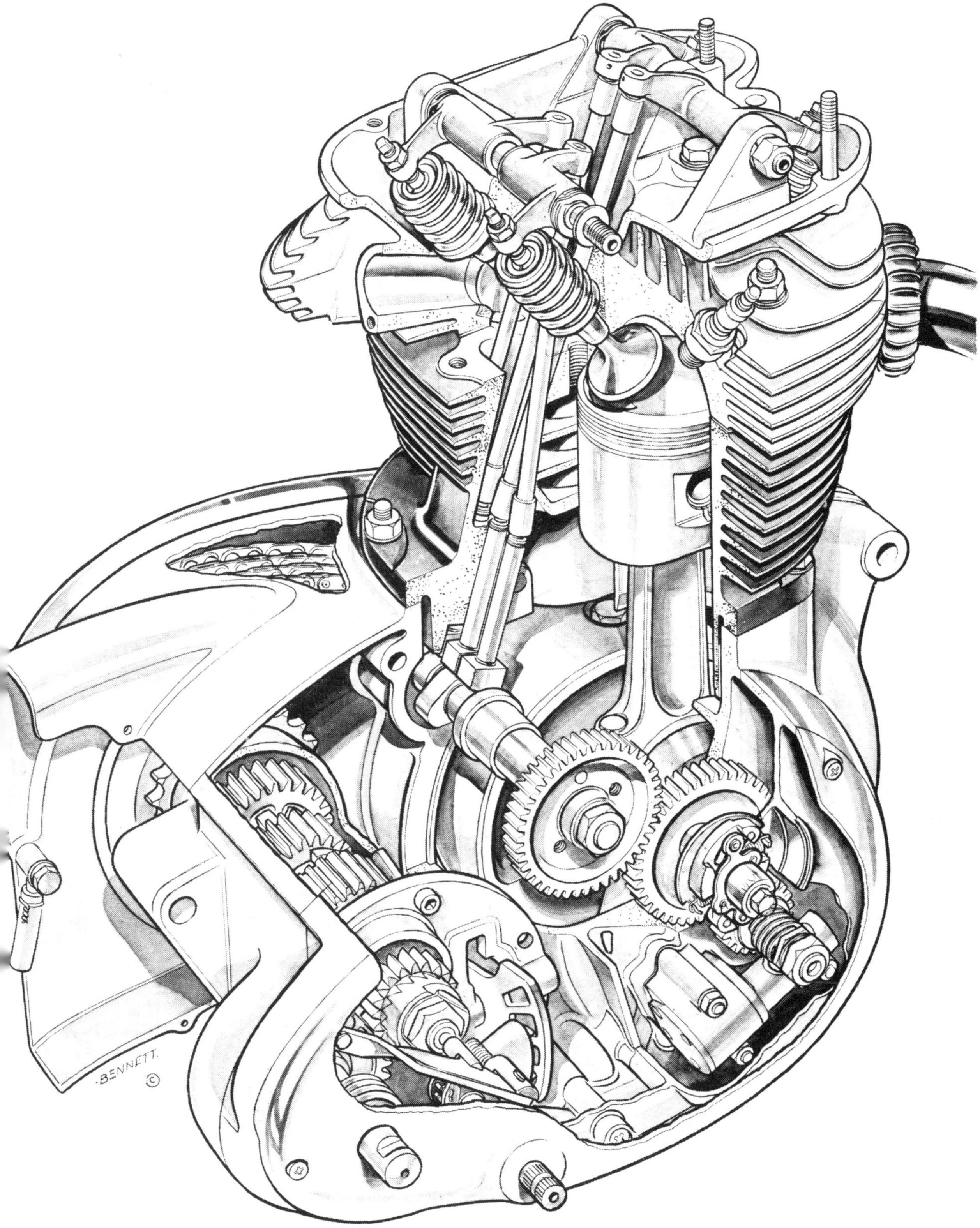
BENNETT
©

52bhp somewhat stressful. If they give up some very strange things start to happen when you change gear, but this is usually not as exciting as one or more of the three bolts which secure a Norton's hub to the rear brake drum coming adrift.

A plethora of Nyloc nuts are to be discovered on both machines. They go a long way to explaining the distinct lack of mobile disassembly one normally associates with 360-degree vertical twins. Not that their addition stops the manual ordering you to check all nuts and bolts for tightness every 2,000 miles. You are also requested to "examine the auto-advance unit" at the same interval, presumably to check that it's still there. With generous flooding and a closed air lever, the bikes fired up first or second kick and the 12-volt lights are more than passable.

Both unit twins began life with full-width hub brakes which must have been mighty ineffectual for David Dixon of *Motor Cycle* to welcome in 1967 the Gold Star type fitted as 'one of the best things that ever happened to the A65.' The front brakes on these two machines are the same 8in single-leading-shoe affair a mere two and a half inches wide, but featuring six large ventilation holes at the back of the drum. We were less than impressed by the brakes' performance. The front one lacked any real feel. I'd hate to have to pull up a heavy combination using these, but an emergency crash-stop yielded a tyre-squealing halt. When the 1968 range was announced, BSA-Triumph had come up with an 8in twin-leading-shoe front brake for the Lightning and that fastest and most fragile of A65 models, the Spitfire. It was a Meriden product, and long overdue. You cannot fit it to early unit twins, however, unless you bring the forks too, as they have Triumph-type axle clamps.

The A65 was never a real success as a competition engine, any more than the A10, ignoring a couple of freak wins. The first A65 of 1962 was a single carb model that could barely scrape 99mph through the timing lights and so the Rocket Gold Star and Super Rocket lingered until a hotter, A65R, version came along. Sidecar racers like Chris Vincent and the Hanks family persevered with a largely hopeless task. Only on the US ovals did the torque of the twins ever make them amount to much in the hands of riders like Dick Mann.

One thing seems to be generally agreed: run one of these engines hard for any length of time and they break. They're not fragile in a 250cc Starfire way, but respond to high revs — and that's *anything* over 6,500rpm, despite BSA's optimistic safe limit of 7,250rpm — by throwing conrods in a quite spectacular fashion. With plain big ends and a crankshaft supported on rollers at the drive side and a plain bush at the other, it's a wise man who keeps his oil fresh and ear cocked for warning noises. Rocker gear seems to suffer a fairly rapid decline despite a direct oil feed to the first plain

The Lightning was a sporty version of the A65 theme, something hinted at by the rev-counter drive.

The Royal Star, though outwardly very similar, is in a much softer state of tune, and sweeter for it.

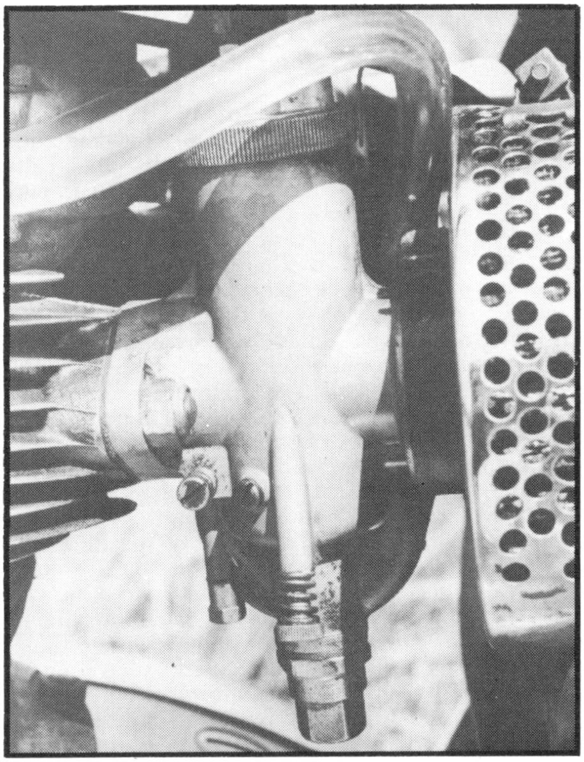

It was said that owners of twin carb BSAs needed a factory fitter to keep them synchronised!

A single concentric keeps the Star fed with fuel, with a cleaner top end response than a Monobloc.

and later finned rocker box. You have to remove the whole thing to adjust the clearances and wield a pushrod 'comb' to get all the pushrods going into the right cups when you're slipping the barrels back on.

Completing most of our test mileage on the 500 Royal Star — just fit A65 barrels and pistons and 499cc becomes 654 — I struck two fairly common problems. The first was an extensive oil leak on the timing chest joint when the oil pump's ball valve in the sump met up with some foreign matter which made the lubrication system blow off at the nearest point, conveniently situated to waterproof my right leg. This has happened before to the Royal Star and is common enough for the handbook to devote a whole paragraph to its occurrence and cure. Every time you whip off the four nuts that secure the filter housing in the sump remember that 'it is advisable at this time to check that the ball is free on its seating'.

Clutch cables also seem to break on late model BSA twins. The A50 surrendered its nipple to me in West Central London. Now I've ridden over 100 miles, and two-up at that, *sans* clutch cable, but 20 miles across the metropolis solo was more than a trifle harrowing. A call to Owen Bros of Battersea Rise secured the information that they did indeed have a cable for a 1960 Royal Star. But when I arrived — minus, in my haste, the old cable — the '68 cable offered looked as wrong as the 1970 one. Enquiries concerning a 1969 cable proving fruitless, I wandered off with something. It didn't fit, reminding me once more of my rule always to remove the old part, take it along and say, "gimme one of those".

Back at Owen Bros I encountered Derek, who runs the spares department and is credited by some of his grateful clients with second sight and a memory that includes all BSA's part numbers. He identified the cable at once as a '69, but when asked for the three timing cover screws I now needed as I'd had to remove the others with an impact driver, he showed me that these were very definitely of 1968 model type, with the characteristic fine thread used up to 1969. Later, a check through the sales ledger at Porter's Motors revealed that this A50 came into stock in 1968, has a 1968 engine and frame number, but wasn't sold or registered until 1970.

So why the '69 cable which went with a so-called 'quick-release' mechanism at the business end of the clutch cable? The answer probably lies in the number of A50 models BSA sold, which was pretty few. Checking the side panels revealed that the Flamboyant Red is sprayed over blue (the 1967 colour scheme for Royal Stars) which argues for a policy of throwing bikes together with whatever's handy. If you have a '68 or earlier unit twin without the quick release on the cable the thing to do is to cut a hole in the timing cover just over the spot where the cable slots into the clutch arm. Make it exactly the same size as the hole in the top of the petrol tank for the single mounting bolt, as Roger did on his '68 A65T, and you can use the same type of rubber grommet to fill the hole when you're not changing clutch cables. BSA themselves did this on their unit singles and it saves butchering three case screws and removing the right-hand footrest, gear lever and the kickstart — it would be secured with a *cotter pin* — every time your cable gives out.

Obscure technical details apart, there remains the question of which unit twin is the most desirable before I tell you how to split the crankcase. The A50 must lose out pretty badly to any of the 650s. BSA described it as a great 'touring' bike, which is sales patter for 'slow'. It consists of the same weighty cycle parts as the 650s dragged around by a not particularly fast 500. It's economical at 59mpg and fairly quick up to 60mph, struggles to an indicated 80mph and last time this one saw 95 on the clock the primary chaincase gasket blew and oil issued from an overpressurised crankcase. The gent who bought this particular A50 in 1970 traded it in against a Bonneville in 1971, and I know how he felt. If it was mine I'd want to raise the overall gearing considerably and once rebore time came around I'd go for 650 barrels and 7.25:1 pistons.

If that sounds like a "back to A10" prescription, I make no apologies. A Lightning just had the edge on a Thunderbolt — by about 5mph right at the top end — and the short-lived Spitfire certainly looked rather neat when it had that large glass-fibre fuel tank. It came complete with 10:1 pistons, hot cam, alloy rims and other goodies as standard. They were pretty quick, especially in Special form when you got a pair of Amal GP carbs along with a special booklet that told you how difficult they were to tune. If a good Lightning will see 110mph flat on the tank, then a Spitfire should make 117mph. However, BSA variously claimed that the Lightning put out 52 or 55bhp at 7,000rpm and that a Spitfire fitted with twin Concentrics developed 56.5bhp (a nice touch, that final half horse) at 7,250rpm. Informed sources claim that not only will few Spitfires make those sort of revs, but that if they do it won't be for long.

There's little doubt that the Royal Star and Lightning would make good, everyday transport if treated with care and given a little love and affection. Their finish is very durable and such modern amenities as 12-volt electrics are nice. But they do nothing a good A10 won't except maybe cost more to buy and shake a little harder. The equivalent Triumphs are lighter, as quick and more reliable. But they're liable to cost more, too. A good A65 of this vintage should be had for around the £500 mark, while A10s do go for much less. You pay your money and I know which my choice would be.

Both bikes are more suited to touring than back-lane scratching, but the handling is excellent.

Specification

1968 BSA ROYAL STAR A50

ENGINE

Type	ohv parallel twin
Bore x stroke	65.5 x 74mm
Capacity	499cc
Compression ratio	9:1
Carburation	26mm Concentric
Bhp rpm	35 @ 6,250
Primary drive	triplex chain
Clutch	multi-plate, wet
Gearbox	4 speed
Electrical system	12v, 110 watt alternator, 10ah battery, coil ignition
Lighting	50/40w headlamp

DIMENSIONS

Wheelbase	55.5in
Seat height	32in
Ground clearance	5in
Kerb weight	419lb
Fuel capacity	4gal
Tyres	
(front)	3.25 x 19 Dunlop
(rear)	4.10 x 18 Dunlop
Brakes	
(front)	8in sls
(rear)	7in sls

PERFORMANCE

Top speed	90mph (est)
Standing ¼ mile	16.5secs (est)
Fuel consumption	59mpg
Braking from 30mph	30ft
Owner	Porter's Motors, Spalding, Lincs.

1967 BSA LIGHTNING A65L

ENGINE

Type	ohv parallel twin
Bore x stroke	75 x 74mm
Capacity	654cc
Compression ratio	9:1
Carburation	2 x 30mm Monobloc
Bhp rpm	52 @ 7,000
Primary drive	triplex chain
Clutch	multi-plate, wet
Gearbox	4 speed
Electrical system	12v, 110 watt alternator, 10ah battery, coil ignition
Lighting	50/40w headlamp

DIMENSIONS

Wheelbase	55.5in
Seat height	32in
Ground clearance	5in
Kerb weight	423lb (est)
Fuel capacity	4gal
Tyres	
(front)	3.25 x 19 Dunlop
(rear)	3.50 x 18 Dunlop
Brakes	
(front)	8in sls
(rear)	7in sls

PERFORMANCE

Top speed	110mph (est)
Standing ¼ mile	15secs (est)
Fuel consumption	55mpg (est)
Braking from 30mph	30ft
Owner	Porter's Motors, Spalding, Lincs.

350cc Douglas 80 Plus

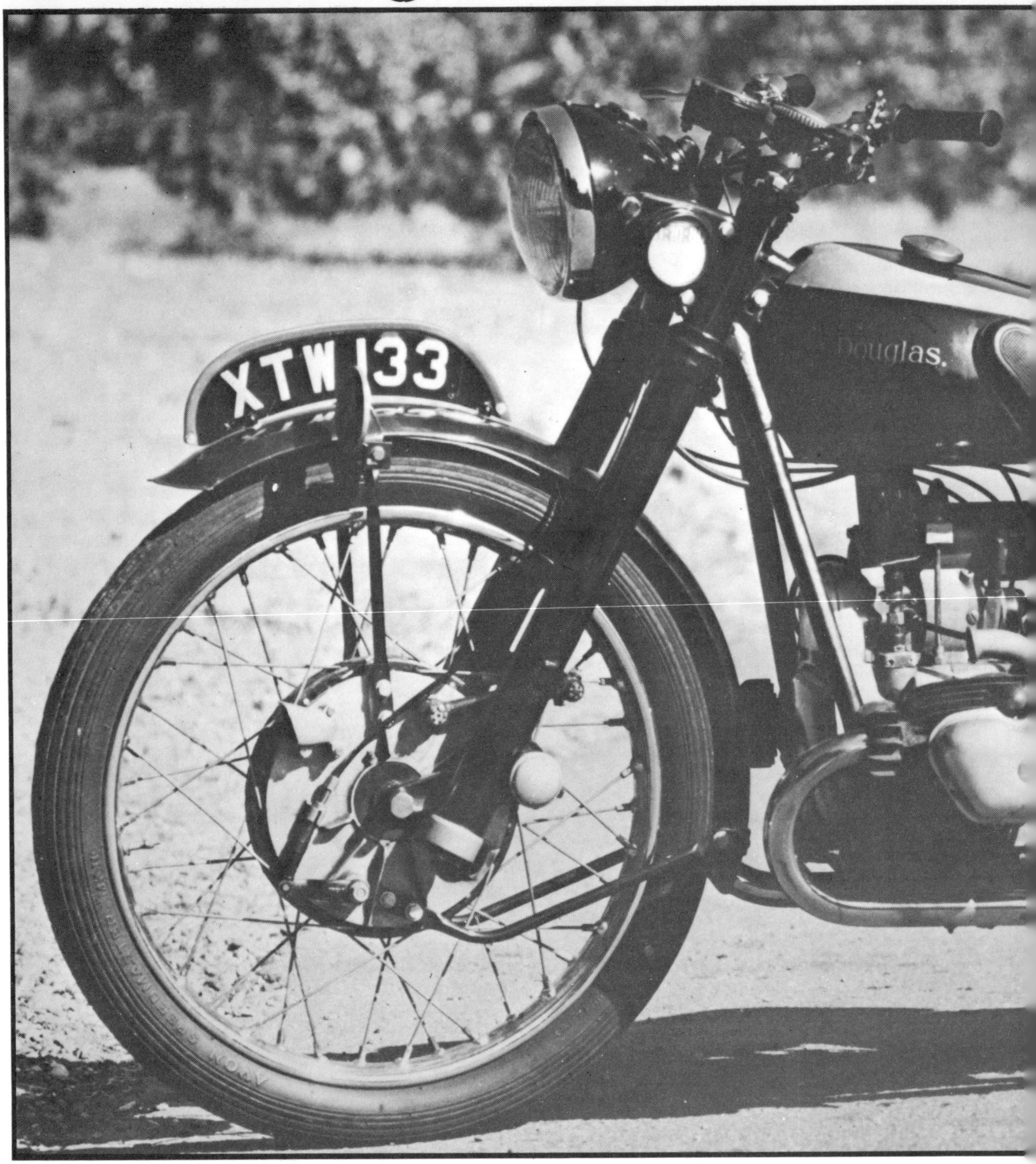

by Peter Watson

Douglas 80 Plus

A couple of years ago I found myself in conversation with that veteran Douglas enthusiast and motorcycle dealer from Godalming, Graeme Brown. We had been discussing the merits and demerits of the post-war Bristol twins, and I thought to ask him why he'd been involved with the marque for over 50 years. Hardly pausing to think, he simply said that he'd started racing and selling Douglas motorcycles because they 'embodied the right principles'.

Now that may seem like a strange thing to say about a marque that was forever plagued by financial difficulties and one which ultimately foundered as a motorcycle producer largely because its machines had become best known for their manifest unreliability. Yet Graeme Brown's viewpoint is entirely justified. For the Douglas flat twins always adhered to the best principles of motorcycle engineering, whether their cylinders lay fore and aft or across the frame. Features such as an excellent power-to-weight ratio, a commendably low centre of gravity, and good handling combined with a horizontally-opposed twin's renowned smoothness are the very embodiment of what most motorcyclists have been looking for since powered two-wheelers took to the highway.

So to say that I jumped at the chance of riding Doug Frost's immaculate 1951 Douglas 80 Plus is something of an under-statement. And yet at the same time I felt a trifle nervous, as memories of my own flirtation with a 1950 Mk V 348cc twin are decidedly mixed. When it went it was everything you could have wished for in a machine of its era: smooth, agile and exciting.

Sadly, this was hardly its normal state. It sulked, refusing to start. It shed nuts, bolts, silencers and parts of its carburettors, and oil issued from every joint. Doug's 80 Plus was so very different: it generated a feeling of quiet satisfaction throughout our weekend together, and we parted the best of friends. Certainly it still has its problems, but the charm of this 80 Plus reveals why examples of the Douglas are so much sought after today, having so singularly failed in their time.

The Mark series models — the T35, Mk III, Mk IV, Mk V, Competition, 80 and 90 Plus — owe the origin of their engine to a World War Two fan-cooled flat-twin generator unit. But although the power source was clearly in step with a whole series of pre-war (and pre-World War One) Douglas models, the chassis was not. Suspension originally was to have been by torsion bar at front and rear, but when the T35 arrived on the British market in 1947 only the rear swinging arm was controlled by that arrangement; a leading-link fork was fitted at the front. The design created an

Low in the frame, the renownedly smooth horizontally opposed engine helped create a low centre of gravity.

Originally intended to be a torsion bar arrangement, production Duggies had leading link suspension.

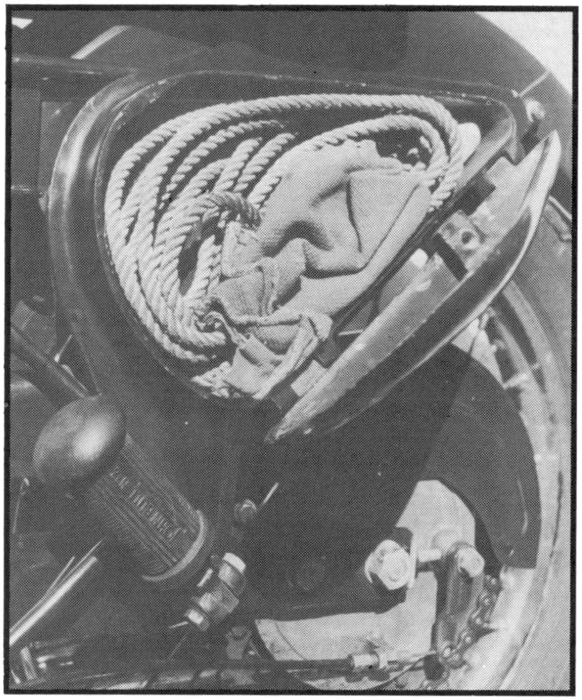

Never ones for cheapness, Douglas saw fit to make the side-boxes from cast alloy.

immediate sensation, but once the public had got its hands on the machine it became apparent that various basic faults had to be remedied at once.

However, by the time *Motor Cycling* got around to testing a Mk III in 1949 Douglas could claim to be the manufacturers of "The fastest '350' sports model on the road today." By any standards, 84mph was really going some for a 'mere' 350. The 80 and 90 Plus models were high-performance variants of the Mk V model and were launched in 1949 as part of an attempt to drag the company out of the financial mess in which, once more, it found itself.

Because the metallic gold 90 Plus — those model numbers relate to a claim of miles per hour 'plus' — was the more glamorous of the two, it has tended to obscure its maroon stablemate. The 90 Plus was available as a production racer at no extra cost, whereas the 80 Plus is merely a fast road machine fitted with much of the 90's equipment. Both are now rare: only 218 90 Plus and 268 80 Plus machines were ever built.

Apart from the colour scheme, the basic difference between standard Mk Vs like mine and the 80 and 90 Plus is to be found in increased power and better braking. The Plus motors were dynamometer tested to see which engines would show over 25bhp. Those which did were destined to be stamped /90, those which failed to make the grade became 80 Plus power plants — all highly scientific stuff by the standard of the period. With a larger (21in) front wheel, more deeply finned cast-iron cylinder heads, a cork-faced clutch with funnel-like air scoop, higher gear ratios, 8.25:1 pistons,15/16in carburettors, and a massive 9in diameter front brake, the 80 Plus may have been technically a reject racer, but it represented a considerable improvement on the Mk V.

The first thing to strike me about this 80 Plus was the curious riding position. You may look at the machine and think how much a sprung saddle would improve its lines, and I would agree. But this guitar-shaped Feridax dual seat was a standard fitting — I had one on my Mk V — despite the mounting lugs for saddle springs that you can spot on the rear sub-frame. This is a spindly, triangulated structure that also supports a pair of superb tear-drop toolboxes cast in aluminium alloy. The 80 Plus is long and low and a sprung saddle would reduce the unladen seat height by three inches to 28in. At first this dual seat makes you feel that you're perched on top of the machine, with the fuel tank way, way below. However, once under way that initial impression is countered by the manner in which the low-slung engine appears to concentrate weight far below the ankles.

With a speed limit of an indicated 60mph set by Doug — "I always feel as if I'm one step away from mechanical disaster," he jokes — I still had the opportunity to rediscover what Douglas handling is all about. Within a few miles the taut, precise feel of the steering had tempted me to pitch the 80 Plus far enough over through a bend to find the sole of my boot contacting tarmac.

Walter Moore's Radiadraulic front fork is a superbly sensitive unit that combines many of the best features of leading-link design. I could fault its action on only two counts: the narrow Plus front mudguard had obviously been clobbered recently by the lower yoke, and a leakage of damping oil (20/50 SAE engine lubricant) was obvious. Although two-way damped, this is one of the Radiadraulic's problems. And under hard braking — the Plus' ventilated ribbed drum being well up to modern road conditions — I felt some slight juddering which I took to be play in the bushes of the brake's two 5.25in parallel torque arms. But how superior this fork is when you compare it to any of the crude telescopics of the period such as the AMC Teledraulic and Norton long Roadholder. It was, and remains, simply years ahead.

One problem associated with all leading-link forks is front mudguard location. On the T35 and Mk III the riddle was solved by using the lower fork yoke as a mounting, which was aesthetically displeasing. The alternative Mk IV and V solution was a floating mounting plate for the mudguard stays designed by M Mouse Engineering. It wore rapidly and rattled alarmingly; the Plus models feature a ribbed alloy casting on the left-hand side which floats properly, allowing the front guard to hug the tyre without actually embracing it!

At the rear, I was once more impressed with the performance of what appears to be a crudely undamped suspension system. Only when faced with a series of vicious bumps taken at 40mph did the rear end momentarily buck me out of the saddle. For the rest of the time it quietly soaked up undulations in a highly satisfactory manner.

The rear fork pivots on two separate bushes, with no spindle connecting them. From above it appears to be a closed box-section unit, but inquisitive fingers reveal that it consists of two stongly crossbrased arms in the form of an inverted U, with solid fork ends. This construction allows free movement to two torsion-bar links, and permits access to the stiff Plus torsion bars, which run the length of the widely splayed lower rails on the duplex cradle chassis. This arrangement is remarkably well engineered, and a great credit to its originator George Halliday, an enthusiastic proponent of torsion-bar springing. The basic flaw in the system is a total lack of damping, other than the frictional damping of the pivot bushes. At least it fools the ignorant, who refuse to believe that the machine has any rear suspension at all . . .

When it's ticking over very slowly, the flat-twin engine will rock the whole machine gently from side to side, much in the fashion of a Moto Guzzi V-twin. This is obviously not very healthy, and in fact is one of the causes of frame cracks on Mark series models, so Doug has set his 80 Plus to idle as a guesstimated 1,000rpm.

The bike pulled strongly from way down the rev range, running especially well in third gear around town. Below 40mph it was pretty pointless slipping up into top, since I felt that I was lugging the engine in such a high gear. A considerable amount of noise from the valve gear was explained by the presence of No 2 cams — a high-lift option that require not less than 25 thou rocker clearance. The two camshafts are gear driven — the only chain employed being for final

The four speed gearbox drives through a single plate clutch – a legacy from the days of shaft drive.

XTW 133
Douglas

With unique but excellently designed suspension front and rear, the Douglas is an exciting bike to ride.

drive — with both the kickstart and gearbox output shafts having their motion turned through 180 degrees. This allows a normal type of kickstart lever to be employed, along the chain final drive. Some whine was apparent from the final drive bevel gears, but the throaty throb of a pair of Burgess silencers was a welcome intrusion.

This machine's worst aspects can be summed up as oil leaks and an appallingly unstable centre stand. Oil mist appeared from around the joint at the base of the gear-driven magdyno, the base flange of each cylinder and from the rev counter drive blanking plate at the front of the crankcase, while gearbox lubricant trickled down the gearchange lever shaft. This last was the most persistent offender and a pad of felt is there to collect the oil; soon an O-ring conversion should stem the flow from the box completely.

As you can see, the oil filler for the sump has been modified to accept a perforated catch-tin which also aids crankcase ventilation to fight off even more oil leaks. I make no apology for leaving this tin in situ during photography; this is a working motorcycle in its everyday trim and, I believe, should be seen as it is, warts and all. A separate dipstick is fitted; the machine used little or no oil in over 150 miles, and fuel consumption worked out at a fairly thirsty 52mpg.

The centre stand is a perfectly ghastly aluminium alloy casting with feet that wear so fast you'd swear they were made of hard cheese painted silver. Doug has had a couple of pads welded on to the feet, but the machine still felt very unstable on some surfaces. Douglas owners have a joke about this stand I first heard years ago. It goes like this: "Why do Douglas owners walk with a limp?" Answer: "Because they've all got housebricks in their jacket pockets to put under the footrest when they want to park." Actually, it never seemed funny at the time . . .

Doug Frost's 80 Plus is a strikingly handsome motorcycle that drew an appreciative audience wherever I went. It starts easily with a little bit of carb tickling and romps away up steep inclines in third gear very strongly. What a delightful production racer the 90 Plus must have made; it's a shame we rarely see one being run hard on a track today.

How would you value this fragile classic? After a weekend I rated it as highly desirable, despite the hair-tearing that my own Douglas caused me. The 80 Plus is a sophisticated little gem, while at the same time being a rorty sporty motorcycle with plenty of character. A British BMW? It might have been, if only the 350s could have been made more reliable and sold cheaply. They were ridiculously overpriced, costing more than 500cc sports twins from other makers like Triumph. A 500cc prototype was built, but never made it into production; the Dragonfly was a styling disaster.

Specification

DOUGLAS 80 PLUS

ENGINE

Type	ohv horizontally opposed twin
Bore x stroke	60.8 x 60mm
Capacity	348cc
Compression ratio	8.25:1
Carburation	2 x 15/16in Amal
Bhp @ rpm	25 @ 7,500 (claimed)
Electrical	Lucas magneto with manual advance/retard, 6v dynamo, 6v battery
Primary drive	direct
Clutch	single plate, car type
Gearbox	4 speed

DIMENSIONS

Frame	duplex tubular
Suspension	
(front)	Radiadraulic leading link
(rear)	swinging arm and torsion bar
Wheels	
(front)	3.00 x 21in
(rear)	3.25 x 19in
Brakes	
(front)	9in sls drum
(rear)	7in sls drum
Wheelbase	55in
Seat height	31in
Ground clearance	5.5in
Dry weight	393lb
Fuel capacity	3gal

PERFORMANCE

Top speed	83-84mph (approx)
Standing ¼ mile	18secs (approx)
Fuel consumption	52mpg
Owner	Doug Frost, publicity officer, London Douglas MCC.

Matchless G12 DeLuxe

by Royce Creasey

Matchless G12

The lovely Matchless G12 De Luxe on test was immediately impressive. It has a rare ability to combine the easy 'big flywheel' feel of a good single at speed with the better engine response and flexibility which are the undoubted advantages of a twin. There are certainly faults in the design — the handling in particular spoils an otherwise excellent open-road performance — but the overall feeling of quality both in operation and detail design calls to mind machines of much wider renown.

Part of this quality is undoubtedly due to a meticulous rebuild, completed in less than a year, by owner Ron Hodson, and his two young sons. The bike's superb finish is merely a reflection of equally thorough mechanical work and, as tested with a comfortable 1,400 miles behind it, I feel that Matchless themselves would have been proud of this G12's condition.

Ron made it clear that he feels the bike is in fact somewhat over-restored and that some engine components could usefully have been left alone. He brought the machine in February 1980 as a complete but tatty garden-shed job with a rough but protective hand-painted finish. Unusually, fringe parts such as mud-guards and lights were still original, but the silencers are a pair made by Unity Equipe to the standard pattern. These modern copies produce a sound every bit as pleasant as the originals, which were a fashionable cafe-racer fitting in the early sixties (so that's where they all went. . .).

Paintwork includes the use of a tricky 'hot spray' polyurethene paint on the frame, although the other cycle parts are cellulose-sprayed. Applied at 100 degrees C, the polyurethene was intended to avoid flaking and chipping when the bike was assembled, but is apparently no better than good stove-enamel. Total purists will also note that the tank badges are pattern plastic rather than the originals, which were missing from the garden shed. All the original plating was renewed, and Ron's sons put in most of the considerable polishing time required to achieve the remarkable finish on the alloy parts. Other details were not neglected, the electrical system and the controls are all in as new condition.

This 1959 650 marks the first year for AMC at this capacity. The bike is a development of the G11 600cc twin, which was in turn a stretch of the original G9 500, introduced in 1949. Apart from the capacity changes the most immediate visible improvement during this period was the adoption of an alloy chaincase in preference to one of those pressed-steel devices with a retaining band, which Velocette owners know so well. Internally, however, considerable work was done on the engine lubrication

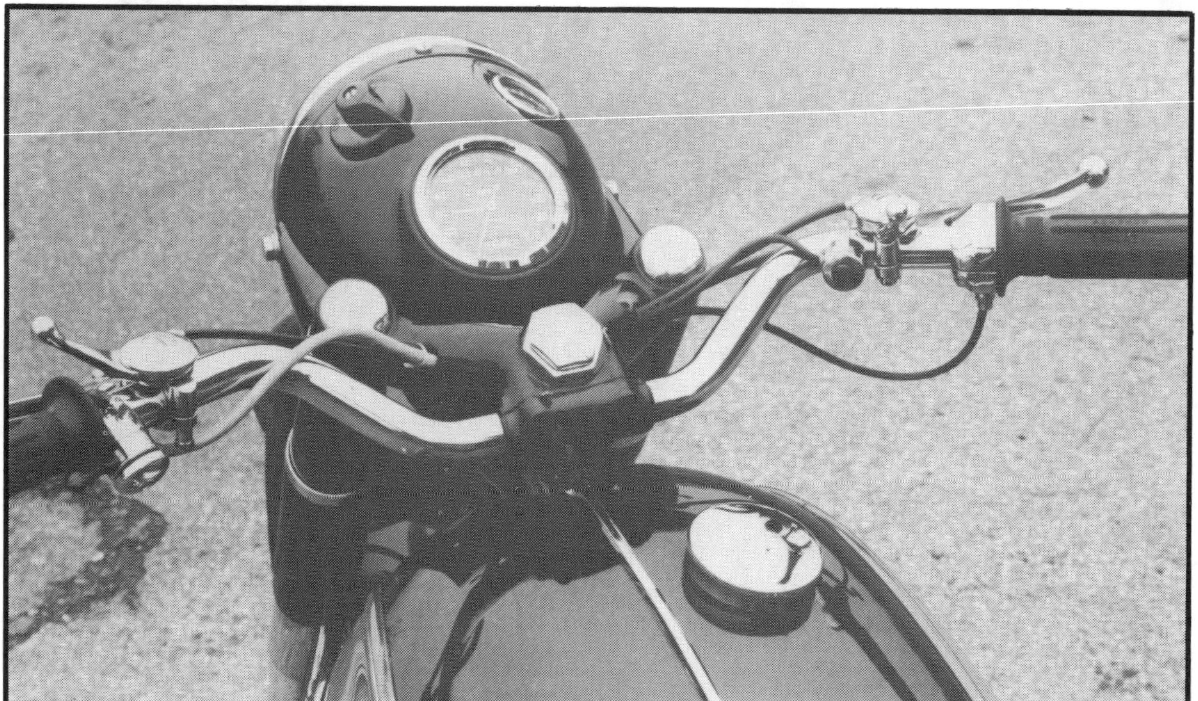

Immaculate restoration shows everywhere, as this G12 shows. Attention to detail has resulted in a handsome bar layout — a place for everything and everything in its place.

Sensitive and progressive, the front brake is pleasant to operate but could use a little more stopping power.

arrangements, which were progressively uprated and improved in a similar fashion to the Royal Enfield system of the same era. Unlike that design the Matchless uses two separate gear-type oil pumps, and includes a small 'short circuit' from the pressure to the scavenge pump to prevent the latter running dry on start-up.

The engine design is also broadly similar to Royal Enfield practice in layout. The camshaft arrangement is similar, although it follows Triumph's policy of driving the cams by gear. But the barrels and heads are separate like the Enfield twins, and it is significant that Matchless also increased the diameter of the retaining studs as their twin grew bigger. The Matchless and (identical AJS) twins, are, however, best known for a unique component in an English parallel twin — a three-bearing crankshaft. This feature is largely responsible for the very restrained vibration felt at normal road speeds on these machines, and the engine does feel exceptionally smooth for a vertical twin.

However the three-bearing shaft, especially the three-bearing crankshaft, is a creature of some sensitivity, and although the original 500 twin was apparently bulletproof, the later 600 and 650cc versions are chiefly notorious for broken crankshafts. Car designers, notably Ford, had overcome this problem by the beginning of the sixties with the introduction of nodular cast iron, a material which could tolerate limited flex without failure, and AMC produced a crank in this material in 1962. I understand that these later cranks are unbreakable, but in any case it seems that failure with the earlier units can be avoided if the engine's high-speed vibration period is avoided.

This vibration period is related to the amount of wear in the plain centre bearing. As the bearing frees, the maximum safe speed increases from about 80mph on the G12 tested (with 1,400 miles clocked) to over three figures by 10,000 miles. Unfortunately the oil supply to the shell-type big-ends relies for its pressure on the condition of the centre main bearing, and rod failures as a result of big-end seizure are not unknown on hardworked examples of this bike.

Away from this somewhat delicate heart the power train feels extremely strong; it will eventually snatch, unlike the trials-oriented Enfield system, but pick-up from very low speeds was remarkably smooth. The engine is damped by a face-cam like other good open road motorcycles, and it's clear that this is the environment most suited to the engine. 'A' road cruising at a very respectable rate was a smooth, half-throttle affair for the motor, with just the right amount of response and engine braking available.

The G12's cycle assembly, despite being built to a high standard of quality and fittings, fails to match the power train in performance. Although excellently balanced as an urban trials bike, the machine has steering geometry which doesn't keep up at speed. A

Matchless G12

top heavy feel is most pronounced in the useful 40 to 60mph range, where it would seem that insufficient turning energy is generated by the geometry to keep the front wheel lined up. I've produced similar effects on other bikes during various maniac experiments, and my misguided guess would be that this geometry needs less rake and more trail. Perhaps some retired member of the Matchless design staff will be able to tell us the real problem.

AMC themselves changed the front end in 1964, fitting Norton Roadholder forks to the AMC frame. Changes to the geometry were made at this time, but it is possible that the Norton forks were chosen simply because they are made up of 37 components to the 55 of the Teledraulics. The fitting of a more responsive modern tyre such as the Avon Roadrunner would help the Teledraulics with the steering today, but in 1959 the handling must have told against this bike when compared with other twins. The 1959 Triumph, for instance, can get into terrible knots if pushed, but it follows a line on its own with reasonable confidence. After a day's run on the Matchless I had to conclude that the steering's uneasy feeling, and the twitching about that resulted from repeated realisation that the bike wasn't pointed quite where I'd aimed it, effectively cancelled many of the G12's outstanding qualities.

The final production G12s must have been fine

Single Monobloc feeds the twin cylinder motor. Potential restorers should note the meticulous polishing here.

Perhaps intended for the mature motorcyclist the 650cc engine was not the most powerful of the multitude of parallel twins spawned in the sixties, but offered smooth torque.

machines, assuming that the suspension change improved the handling, and it is interesting that the factory reacted to the problems which emerged from this design with some dispatch. Even today, troubles persist with modern production motorcycles for three or four years, despite much better technology and rather better media coverage of design failings. But in AMC's case press comment was virtually non-existent throughout the fifties due to the policy of company chief Don Heather.

Apparently outraged by critical reaction to one of his products, he stopped releasing test bikes, and in a response that is incomprehensible to infant upstarts like me, the magazines of the day complied by refraining from simply borrowing machines from private owners. As a result virtually no written history or technical information is available for these machines. It's also true that AMC ceased production of bikes a few years before the more publicity-oriented manufacturers of parallel twins, but from the viewpoint of 1980 it's debatable whether the press ban, with its consequent loss of publicity and appraisal, made much difference to the marque's disappearance.

AMC seem to have intended the G12 for what could be called the mature motorcyclist, a rider able to appreciate quality and refinement, and more interested in easy and rapid touring than all-out speed. The operation of the controls and the seating position all relate well to this ideal. The brakes in particular are impressively sensitive and progressive, ideal for that steadying touch although lacking the power of the later Norton unit. The gearchange is also very easy; neutral at a standstill can be difficult to find with a hot clutch, but the change at speed keeps up nicely with the free-revving engine. Clutch operation mars this quality by being heavy and somewhat slow, but does not spoil the gearchange operation.

Comfort could be improved by fitting Girling Gas shocks, but in standard form the suspension copes adequately and keeps the seat level at speed. The riding position is set for that giant thirteen-stone Briton who seemed to form the bulk of buyers in the fifties, so my 9½ stones were probably insufficient to load the suspension properly. No doubt a suitable load would soften the ride to 'touring' from its current 'sports' level of firmness.

High speed handling leaves something to be desired though the steering is admirably suited to town work.

Another G12 feature that the more experienced rider used to appreciate is a hand-advance magneto, a control that gets used virtually all the time or hardly at all. The Matchless is very responsive to liberal ignition adjustment and can be converted readily from town to country modes simply by swivelling the advance lever. The matching choke lever assists with a cold engine and then, in common with many other English designs, can be immediately opened. Starting when hot, cold or uneasily warm was inevitably a first kick affair. I've never found parallel twins too easy to kick over, but at least this one needs prodding only once.

Apart from the firm ride other criticism can be levelled at details of the machine. The centre stand requires more strength than I would like to muster continuously (Ron would like to hear from anyone who has a sidestand) and the kick-start lever is non-folding. But these are minor complaints and do little to spoil the G12's general quality. Price consideration apart, the Matchless would probably have been compared with the contemporary BMW, and favoured for its traditional design and that dash of English crispness for those fine old 'A' roads.

The press ban may have reduced sales, but may also have prevented public awareness of the engine and handling weaknesses. In the event I do not remember the AMC twin as one of the popular bikes of its time, although there was a passing vogue for the sporting version of the G12, the surprisingly fast CSR. This lack of sales, compared with BSA or Triumph for instance, did not relate to any lack of quality in the AMC twin. It's just that in 1959 its intended 'mature' customer was probably running a Ford Anglia (that other device with a nodular iron crank), while parallel twin enthusiasts of the day were primarily interested in which design would go fastest for longest. History records that in the end it was a close tie between Triumph and Norton, but at that time Triumph made the quick engine that stayed in one piece (for a while) and the AMC twin that mainly broke first was ignored by the young riders of the period.

Looked at today, the G12 deserves a place among the better English designs. Its two major faults seem curable and are well understood, while on quality alone the Matchless rates ahead of other parallel twins from this country. This is the one that doesn't feel like a tractor, that doesn't seem to have rubber connecting either the transmission or the frame. In my fashion I would immediately start to experiment with the handling, and probably fit the one-tooth higher CSR gearing to push that deadly vibration period even higher up the speed range until I managed to lay hands on the nodular crank. As it is, this bike can be compared in its better aspects to other makes which are not even parallel twins. Velocette and Vincent, for instance.

Specification

1959 MATCHLESS G12 DE LUXE

ENGINE

Type	ohv parallel twin
Bore x stroke	72 x 79.5mm
Capacity	646cc
Compression ratio	7.5:1
Carburation	Amal Monobloc
Bhp @ rpm	n/a
Electrical	Lucas K2F hand-control magneto, 6v 60w Lucas dynamo/regulator
Primary drive	single-row chain
Clutch	multi-plate, wet
Gearbox	4 speed

DIMENSIONS

Frame	single downtube, cradle type
Suspension	
(front)	AMC Teledraulic telescopic fork
(rear)	Swinging arm and AMC struts
Wheels	
(front)	3.25 x 19in
(rear)	3.50 x 19in
Brakes	
(front)	sls drum
(rear)	sls drum
Wheelbase	55.5in
Seat height	31.5in
Ground clearance	5.5in
Dry weight	394lb
Fuel capacity	3.75gal

PERFORMANCE

Top speed	105mph (est)
Standing ¼ mile	15.5secs (est)
Fuel consumption	60mpg
Owner	Ron Hodson, Bristol

Norton Dominator Model 7

by Peter Watson

Norton Dominator

It's pretty fashionable these days to knock the parallel twin, forgetting both what it replaced — the universal single — and just how different those first lowly stressed engines were from their descendants.

A couple of weeks with Tony Wilkins' 1953 Norton Dominator Model 7 made it obvious why Norton's first twin (discounting the early Peugeot engine) was such a success from its launch in 1948 in 29bhp, 497cc form, to its demise as the 58bhp, 828cc Commando in 1977.

It felt remarkably smooth — up to 55mph — amazingly torquey and pretty quick for a 25-year-old 500. Certainly the ride and comfort were not up to modern standards, but the steering had that precise, Norton feel. Small and good looking, with a seat height of just over 30 inches, it must have been a revelation after all those singles.

You don't see many Model 7 Nortons around these days, largely because it was so soon overshadowed by the first Featherbed framed roadster twin. Launched at Earls Court in 1951, the Dominator 88 was still 'for export only' in 1953 when the first Dominator had just been fitted with swinging arm rear suspension.

It had started out life with a plunger-sprung frame that was the old Norton rigid chassis rapidly modified around its rear end. With a new frame already in production, the Model 7 had its swinging arm added in the same fashion. It says a lot for the basic design that it was able to cope with these assaults.

The only problems I encountered were front wheel patter over 80mph, occasional topping out from the Armstrong suspension units at the rear, and the inevitable grounding that results from fitting modern tyres to an older bike and then riding it to the limit.

And, of course, tyres aren't the only things that have changed dramatically since 1953; road conditions are altogether different. Twenty-five years ago the average family car cruised along 45mph if that, while your average Model 7 owner probably never worried about the 360 degree twin's vibration because he rarely went fast enough for it to begin gradually disassembling the machine. The headlamp-mounted light switch disappeared during my first 40 miles, and after that I went over the whole bike with a spanner in faultless '50s-style maintenance manual fashion.

Only the brakes really gave me a scare. As the 1949 *Motor Cycle* test observed, the front brake

A mass of wires and cables, the Model 7's handlebar layout is truly of its time.

The front brake is far too small to provide safe stopping, but the forks are excellent.

"...never quite came up to recognised Norton standard". As you'd imagine, that was putting things rather mildly. The 7 x 1¼in drum was totally inadequate by today's standards and I went back to relying on anticipation and a good deal of engine braking.

The Dominator engine was mainly the work of Bert Hopwood — who also designed the 250 Norton Jubilee, we all make mistakes — with Norton's chief designer J. E. Moore. Hopwood had recently been working for Triumph and might have been reasonably expected to use his inside knowledge of the 1937 Edward Turner Speed Twin's faults to improve the Norton.

Great emphasis was placed on cooling, with wide-splayed exhaust ports in the one-piece cast iron head and rocker box. And despite its later problems, Norton twin owners were doubtless grateful for the fact that the pushrod tunnels were cast into the block, rather than suffer the famous Triumph pushrod tube oil leak.

As suggested by its power output, the Model 7 came in a low state of tune. Part of this was due to the 'pool' fuel of the period, the doubtful combustion qualities of which came from an octane rating of around 70. Thus the compression ratio of 6.75:1,

Rear mudguard is hinged to allow easy removal of the standard quickly detachable wheel.

"which we think is as high as we can go on pool petrol", said J. E. Moore.

The flat-topped pistons have tiny valve cutouts due to the very shallow heads and the cam is obviously extremely mild, making it a very flexible motor. With these disadvantages compounded by a small 1in Amal carburettor, the Dominator had a lot of tuning potential.

Other features were pretty standard for the period: plain big ends with detachable shells, light alloy forged conrods, Lucas K2F magneto and 6v dynamo situated on either side of the block and chain driven, a single-row primary chain and separate gearbox.

The pressed-steel primary chaincase, which Norton retained for so long, is usually the major source of oil leaks although this one was a good fit. The engine instead dribbled from the rocker feed take-off banjo by the oil tank and old gaskets on the three rocker-box inspection covers needed replacing.

A high whirring from the engine immediately reminded me of how careful you have to be setting up the chain tension with a separate box which you move backwards and forwards to adjust the primary chain. It was as tight as a bowstring, and having slack-ened off the two through bolts that hold the gearbox rigidly in the frame, I wound the threaded adjuster back only to be mystified by the fact that the box didn't seem to want to move very far forward. Naturally it won't when you have the final drive chain as tight as the primary once was... So off I went round to the rear spindle to slacken off the rear chain, tensioned the primary — careful to take up any slack on the kickstart before finally locking the gearbox up again — and moved back to readjust the final drive.

A prolonged and frequently infuriating business if you don't know how, but not as bad as removing the rear wheel of a modern bike fitted with an endless chain. The Norton came equipped with the once-traditional three-bolt quickly detachable rear wheel which leaves the chain and sprocket drum undisturbed.

Along with the usual odd-looking collection of equipment by modern standards — toolbox, steering damper, massive and feeble Lucas horn, battery hanging out in the weather — the Norton came equipped with some really useful items as standard.

An ammeter is always nice to have, especially as the battery takes such a pounding from vibration. The rear one-piece stay on the front mudguard is also a stand for easy front-wheel removal. The rear mudguard and chain guard provide plenty of protection for your passenger and transmission, while the rear guard also hinges up to let the rear wheel out. And unlike other manufacturers — who usually put it under the seat — Norton mounted the CVC voltage-control unit for the charging circuit inside the toolbox out of the wet.

Tony Wilkins' bike is by no means all original as many of you will have already noticed. Most obviously it isn't fitted with the correct and extremely ugly flattened-pear shaped silencers. Likewise it has later control levers, passenger footrests and

More 'Garden Gate' then Featherbed, the Model 7 nevertheless can be ridden quickly and safely.

front and rear lights. The model 7 fuel tank, a highly individual piece of design, should also be chromed, although the black-lined silver enamel panels are perfectly correct.

Not that all this and more that is not original really detracts from the bike's looks at all. And I consider that while some people naturally want a restored machine to be flawlessly accurate, this takes no account of the changes that owners naturally made over the years. This is no museum piece just left to sit in the showrooms of Ken Ives Ltd in Leicester where Tony Wilkins is managing director, it's meant to be used and runs extremely well.

What strikes you most about the Model 7 is its superb exhaust note, orchestrated by a throaty rasp from the carb's bellmouth that breaks into a full-blooded roar when you really wind it on. Flat out through the timing lights at 88.23mph — *Motor Cycle* achieved 92mph in 1949 — it felt good and sounded better.

The advantages of owning a machine like the Model 7 are its comparative rarity matched by the fact that it makes completely reliable everyday transport. You just flood the separate float chamber Amal and kick for it to fire up, while it will hold 60 or 65mph all day if you can stand the tingling vibration as the Smiths chronometric speedo — which reads left to right — ticks accurately back and forth.

There are the little things to learn, of course. The gearbox has a one-up-and-three-down pattern matched by a delightfully light clutch and as the lever travel is extensive it pays to take your time to avoid the slight scrunch felt on a really snappy change.

Rather surprisingly, the bike's lock is very poor which feels strangely at odds with the overall handling. The friction steering damper can only have been fitted with sidecar work in mind — the frame is equipped with mounting lugs — and I kept it slackened off the whole time.

One of the nicest things about the bike was its state of tune. It would pull through town happily at 30mph in top and then build up to 70 in an amazingly short distance without changing gear. It felt relaxed and relaxing, with a comfortable riding position, but quite up to being thrashed a series of tight curves just for the hell of it.

I really enjoyed the Model 7 in every way. Just looking at it, working on it, riding it for a few hundred miles and wanting to ride it more. Yet it seemed to bear such little resemblance to the Norton twins I've ridden in the past.

It was nothing like the race-tuned 600cc 99 that would make 120mph with its Quaife five-speed gearbox and manhole-cover valves. And as for a Commando — there's hardly a comparison. In many ways Norton's first twin was perhaps their best.

Specification

NORTON DOMINATOR

ENGINE

Type	ohv parallel twin
Bore x stroke	66 x 72.6mm
Capacity	497cc
Compression ratio	6.75:1
Carburation	1in Amal
Bhp @ rpm	29 @ 6000
Primary drive	single row chain
Clutch	Multiplate, wet
Gearbox	4 speed
Electrical system	Lucas magneto with auto advance. Separate 45w Lucas dynamo

DIMENSIONS

Wheelbase	58in
Seat height	30.5in
Overall width	28.5in
Ground clearance	6in
Kerb weight	418lb (inc 1gal fuel)
Fuel capacity	3.75gal
Tyres	
(front)	3.25 x 19 Dunlop K70
(rear)	4.10 x 10 Dunlop TT100
Brakes	
(front)	7 x 1¼in drum
(rear)	7 x 1¼in drum

PERFORMANCE

Top speed	
(prone)	88.23mph
(sitting up)	83.33mph
Standing ¼ mile	17.51sec
Speedometer error	
at indicated 30mph	29.91mph
at indicated 60mph	58.02mph
Fuel consumption	
overall	55mpg
ridden hard	52mpg
Braking distance	
from 30mph	55ft
from 60mph	126ft
Supplied by	Ken Ives Ltd, 220 Loughborough Road, Leicester

250cc OK Supreme Model SV/39

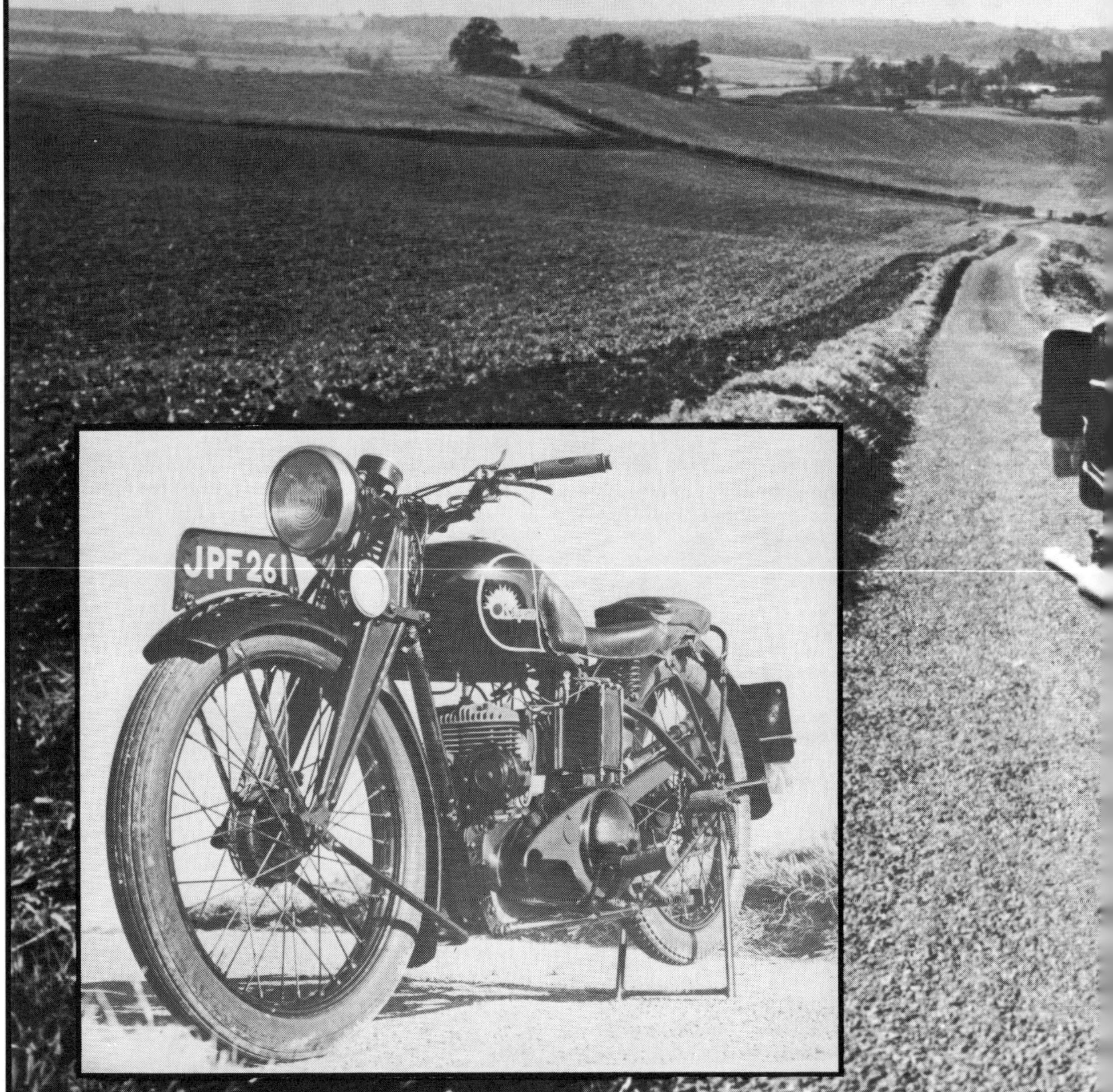

by Val Ward

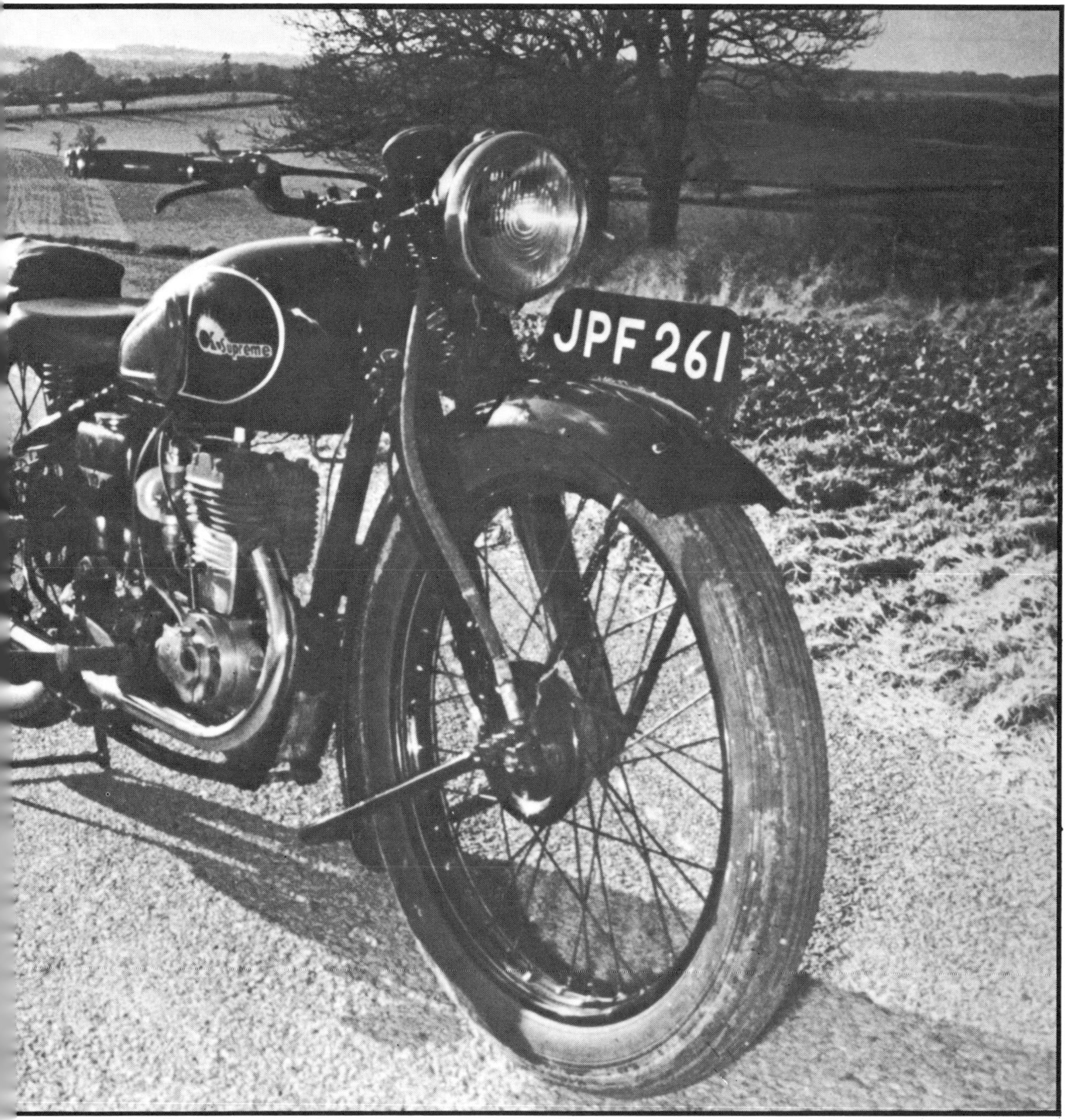

OK Supreme

Expensive thoroughbreds can be shameless glory-grabbers. Fussed over and kept for special occasions, they need be seen but briefly to stay in the memory for a lifetime while mass-produced bikes pass unnoticed, most doomed by their very cheapness to be ridden into the ground. This is about a workhorse that escaped the knacker's yard.

When this survivor, a 1939 250cc sidevalve OK Supreme, surfaced two years ago at an auction three things prompted Tony Wilkins to buy it. He was told it was in completely original condition, it ran very well and according to the odometer it had covered less than 600 miles from new. The vendor's explanation was that the first owner fell off in 1941 and immediately put the bike in store, where it remained undisturbed until 1978.

If the story is true, and nothing has been found to contradict it, JPF 261 is that rarity, a high-fidelity mirror of what was available pre-war to riders wanting economical transport. So it deserves careful assessment.

In terms of general performance the Model SV/39 might be called — excuse the comparison — the Honda Ninety of its day. At £38 17s 0d all in, it was OK's bargain-basement special in a range of thirteen singles which included two ohc designs, the rest having pushrod-operated overhead valves. There were, however, cheaper 250s.

The motorcycle market in this country in the late thirties was highly competitive, and many makers produced cut-price bikes to boost sales charts and mollify company accountants. New Imperial made a 250cc utility solo for seven shillings less than the OK, the simplest Royal Enfield cost but £35 and Wolf's 249cc WA Eleven was just £33 17s 0d. Undercutting them all, AJW and Panther shared the doubtful honour of making the lowest-priced quarter-litre bikes then available in Britain — spartan lightweights each selling for only £29 17s 6d.

In this sector of the market, the side-valve OK was up against some cheeky, rather primitive two-strokes and many ruthlessly simplified ohv four-strokes. It held two winning cards: proven reliability, and long-term economy. The OK might have given the opposition a still harder time had the Birmingham company deleted such frills as red pinstriping from the black-enamelled wheels and fitted one stand instead of two

The side-valve engine puts out a lowly 10bhp, but returns a remarkable 140mpg on two star petrol.

Simple but rugged, the 249cc JAP unit offers reliable, economic and rather unexciting riding.

and thus reduced the price. But OK liked to do things with a flourish as their 1939 range, announced the previous August, testified: arguably the finest machine in it was an ohc two-fifty with an engine that was all their own work.

The test bike, obviously rugged, was until recently a closed book to Tony Wilkins as no descriptive literature accompanied it. But two great classic machine enthusiasts, Eddie Collin of South Witham in Lincolnshire, and the Vintage club's OK marque specialist, Michael Nichols of Penryn in Cornwall, solved the puzzle. They turned up details of the mechanical specification and much besides about the company's history.

John Humphries and Jack Davis jointly supervised OK's Hall Green production line until a row led to Humphries' departure. Contrary to popular belief, OK between 1928 and 1930 also controlled another famous name — HRD — having acquired the business from its disillusioned founder Howard R. Davies before Philip Vincent took over.

The soft JAP engine that OK preferred for their bread-and-butter 250 began in 300cc form with bore and stroke dimensions of 70 x 78mm, and was further detuned for longevity when they specified a 64.5 x 76mm barrel for the same bottom half; among others Cotton and Zenith fitted the same unit. The cylinder head is detachable and a bolt-on cover, quickly removable, encloses valve stems and springs.

Tank and side-panel badges were recreated faithfully, using photographs of the originals for guidance.

Dunlop saddle is the long lasting original.

OK Supreme

Total-loss oiling, governed by an adjustable Pilgrim pump on the offside, serves an uncaged roller-bearing big-end, drive-side rollers, and on the timing side a plain bronze bush. One modification is a long, rather imprecise foot-change lever for the Burman three-speed 'box, ratios being 6:1, 9.8:1 and 16:1.

With a 4.8:1 compression ratio and at most 10bhp at about 5,000rpm, the engine provides the sort of acceleration which, to be kind, one might term leisurely. Rapid pick-up is foreign to the OK's nature, however, for its strength lies at the lower end of the scale. This means that once above 15mph on a flat road the rider need never change out of top, since the standard third-gear ratio copes admirably with the stiffest head wind, the secret being the sort of torque steam engines boast.

Fairly low, with a seat height meant to please short-legged riders, the OK is also quite light and ready to roll scales just 260lb — half a hundredweight less than many a modern 250. This helps it to do well on its modest power output: slow but sure, the OK stays unruffled in the fiercest weather and doggedly plods on.

Many items on the bike certainly look authentic. In keeping with the claimed background are such apparently original fittings as a Britton tyre pump, front wheel-driven Smiths 0-90mph speedometer with resettable trip distance recorder, tiny Amal carburettor with separate float chamber and wiremesh grit trap, 300 x 20 tyres, voltage regulator below the seat and John Bull kneegrips.

Other features that seem right include a twistgrip having a cable fed through the handlebar, a triangular toolbox, ignition by battery and coil, and an old-fashioned clip holding the ht lead to an 18mm Lodge plug. The end of the handlebar clutch lever has been broken off.

The frame, adequate but not glaringly substantial, comprises a single top tube, a single downtube, a duplex cradle for the engine and gearbox and four tubes which sweep back from a seat buttress rail to the wheel spindle slots. An intermediate strut supports the gearbox, which pivots for primary chain adjustment. Grease is used to lubricate the 'box as the six-volt chain-driven magdyno, linked to it, won't tolerate oil. Running at engine speed, the ignition system produces an ideal spark.

The OK, undemanding from cold, is generally easy to control, straightforward to maintain and trouble free. A touch of luxury comes from a wide Dunlop Drilastic saddle — in my view the neatest and best motorcycle single seat ever made. Of thick moulded rubber, these seats were available in three sizes, 15-inchers being supplied for Broughs and other large-capacity machines, 13-inch versions for 350-500cc bikes and 11-inch types for lightweights.

Light steering, poor forks and brakes and a barely adequate frame detract from the OK's supremity.

What makes them particularly attractive is something they don't have, ie networks of backside-nipping springs found in mattress saddles. Supple yet strong, Dunlops hold their shape indefinitely so long distances can be covered non-stop without fatigue. Their heyday was the thirties, when hard riders of machines with no rear suspension prized them. After the war Bert Greeves used them on his trials springers and they enjoyed a short vogue in the fifties, many being fitted to tractors used in the controversial ground-nut scheme. Now as rare as gold dust at the North Pole, these saddles are well worth tracking down, and I wouldn't have any other kind on my own pre-war solo. The one on the OK is in places cracked with age, but still has plenty of life in it.

Pristine Raleigh pillion footrests, available as extras when the bike was new, are teamed with another period touch, a cushioned oblong pad on the mudguard. A passenger truly floats on air, the pad being inflatable.

Bumps don't exactly disappear but spine-jarring shocks are the exception, thanks to a level of comfort which for a rigid-frame machine is very good. Complementing it are sturdy pressed-steel girder forks — another cost-cutting ploy — and within their limitations they work well. However, poor roads make them dance and show up the lack of effective damping.

Other shortcomings are incredibly light steering that demands care and veers from the chosen path if the rider so much as coughs, and a puny front brake. There appeared to be nothing wrong with the bits and pieces involved, but OK were surely asking a lot of a five-inch drum with miniscule linings. Dragging one's feet on the road might stop this 60-mph bike faster. The six-inch rear drum, operated by a thick rod, was much better at slowing the machine.

Roadholding seemed no better than fair, though tricky steering colours the verdict. The lights do work, but I was glad all test riding was done by day as the six-inch headlamp, checked at noon, produced a discouraging yellow beam.

Modest running costs redress the balance. The OK's low compression ratio was chosen to suit 70-octane fuel at a time when better grades were scarce. It's still a good penny-saver, doing about 140mpg. Oil consumption averages 1,500mpg.

Tony Wilkins, who runs a motorcycle business in Market Harborough, has had to spend little to keep the bike roadworthy, save for a respray for the three-gallon tank which had rusted. Dream Machine of Station Road, Beeston, Nottingham did the work and faithfully recreated side panel emblems from photographs.

A vexing problem remains. How can Tony use the bike as often as he would like without spoiling its low-mileage appeal? Fortunately, he is not short of something to ride. He has twenty other machines.

Specification

1939 OK SUPREME MODEL SV/39

ENGINE

Type	**side-valve single**
Bore x stroke	**64.5 x 76mm**
Capacity	**249cc**
Compression ratio	**4.8:1**
Carburation	**$\frac{7}{8}$in Amal**
Bhp @ rpm	**10 @ 5,000**
Electrical	**6v battery and coil chain-driven dynamo**
Primary drive	**single-row chain**
Clutch	**multi-plate**
Gearbox	**3-speed, foot-change**

DIMENSIONS

Frame	**tubular**
Suspension	
(front)	**pressed steel girders**
(rear)	**none**
Tyres	
(front)	**300 x 20 Dunlop ribbed**
(rear)	**300 x 20 Firestone studded**
Brakes	
(front)	**5in sls drum**
(rear)	**6in sls drum**
Wheelbase	**50in**
Seat height	**26in**
Ground clearance	**6in**
Weight	**260lb**
Fuel capacity	**3gal**

PERFORMANCE

Top speed	**60mph (est)**
Standing $\frac{1}{4}$ mile	**25secs (est)**
Fuel consumption	**140mpg**
Oil consumption	**1,500mpg (est)**
Owner	**Tony Wilkins, Market Harborough, Leics.**

250cc Royal Enfield Continental GT

by Royce Creasey

Royal Enfield Continental

About half-way through this test I suddenly had this vision. Nothing too spiritual, you realise, in fact the vision concerned the boardroom of the Royal Enfield motorcycle company, some time around mid-1964. A group of serious businessmen are gathered to consider the market for their various motorcycles. It is decided that something that will appeal to the youth market is in order, and, it being 1964, this means a cafe racer. You can imagine the slightly disconcerted silence that follows the chairman's question, "Just what exactly *is* a cafe racer?"

Then some younger member of the firm, possibly one of these new-fangled marketing types, comes forward a little hesitantly, and explains his version: "You take any motorcycle and remove everything not actually crucial to either going or stopping, including effective silencing. Then you tune the motor to the point where it's about to go bang, and fit an excruciatingly uncomfortable combination of rear-sets and clip-ons, usually without altering the seat height." So they went and did that, and at the same time noticed that there were various fashionable goodies, invariably functionless, that were essential to the cafe racer concept. These got included too.

Naturally, this was a somewhat speculative venture, aimed at catching a fickle and uncertain specialist market. Therefore, costs had to be minimal, and it clearly made sense to start work on the cheapest end of the Enfield range, the cooking but useful Crusader. The Continental GT featured in this test was the end result. In original condition except for the seat, which is cunningly set even higher than on the standard bike, it's got everything the young provisional licence holder was considered to dream about. By 1964 I'd held a full licence for all of three years, and had consequently developed the deep wisdom and clear perception that allowed me to see through the Continental's swept-back exhaust, tachometer, and fibre-glass tank, to the mere 250 that lurked within. In addition, I was running the real Royal Enfield cafe racer — the stripped-down 350 Bullet. Such are the delusions of assumed maturity.

In detail, Royal Enfield do not appear to have skimped on their official version of the cafe racer. The GT's motor runs the highest state of tune of any of the 250 range; there's a 9.5:1 compression ratio, a big carb, lumpy cams, and a bloodline set at a scary 7,500rpm. Bear in mind that in those days a bloodline *was* a bloodline, the point beyond which the engine would break. The model also came with the notorious Enfield five-speed gearbox fitted, and though I find it difficult to believe, the company apparently supplied a complete four-speed cluster with each bike. Rear-sets were specially made, and in true Enfield tradition

Produced for only two years the Continental GT was one of the snappiest numbers of its era – an English Ducati.

Developed from the 14bhp Clipper motor, the 26 bhp unit has an alloy head and 9.5:1 compression.

An ample supply of breathers gives the engine a purposeful look – and helps keep oil inside the cases.

are strong enough to operate an earth mover. Closely following the correct cafe racer tradition, the cycle itself was left unmodified, but stripped of toolboxes and heavy mudguards, and equipped with that rather pretty plastic tank.

This reduction in weight resulted in the rear suspension being too hard, but that's what cafe racers were like. At the front it would hardly have been practical to fit worn-out forks with shot damping, so they did the next best thing and affixed sufficiently flexible forks which had no damping at all. Company tradition left them unable to design a snappy top yoke, so the amazing Casquette got distorted again to allow for a racy headlight shell and the twin-dial instrument layout. The useless wheel discs — 'bacon slicers', as they were called — were the hottest fashion at the time, being copied from one of the real racers (was it Petty or Arter? 7R or Manx?). If they had been bolted firmly to some monstrous double-drum brake, they might have actually been useful on the Enfield. The swept-back exhaust had appeared before on the Crusader Sport, but of course was cribbed from the BSA Gold Star. On the street an imitation Gold Star silencer was almost mandatory for Continental GTs, so you'll have to overlook the rather modern annual discharge unit fitted to the test bike. You will be reassured to know, however, that it's just as noisy. I feel that the exhaust is perhaps the only component that doesn't look right on the test machine — it hangs too low, but in fact doesn't ground. This job is left to the centre stand, and unlike the situation on most Enfields, when this one scrapes the dated tyres means that you really are trying. The lighting is surprisingly complete, and the neat battery box was one of the early samples of plastic covers.

This particular bike has a history worthy of its presumed class. Its year of manufacture can only have been either '65 or '66, which formed the brief production run of this model, but its official history starts in '77 when it was re-registered, having been built from the bits left after a lorry had run over it. About five months later the four-speed cluster was fitted, and another five-speed gearbox got dustbinned. Then a minor foreign object operated on the oil system, the Achilles heel of this engine, and caused a violent seizure. Violent enough, that is, to break the rod and ruin both maincases. Fortunately this is another Royal Enfield that lives within striking distance of L & D Motors of Bristol, the Enfield people in the area. Once again the bike got rebuilt, this time incorporating several more correct bits and the standard late-seventies electrics — 12 volts, zener diode and a real

Royal Enfield Continental

rectifier. When I collected it, it had been run for about 1,500 miles and was beginning to look like this time it meant it. A nice touch of traditional class was the slightly bent left-hand clip-on.

I'd already thought about the Continental GT's impact on us bikers back there in the sixties, and remembered that although it was cheap and looked rather nice, the 250 Ducati did the same job better, while the Honda Dream, with 12 volts and electric starting allied to overhead cam valve-gear and twin cylinders, did the job in a different fashion altogether. I decided that the Enfield would have appealed to the youth who wanted but couldn't afford the Duke, or who bled for a Gold Star, but had first to pass a driving test. His typical pattern would have been to barely use the thing during the week, and then go for a prolonged thrash over the weekend, hopping from cafe to cafe along the A and B roads of the day. This, then, was the course I decided on as the basis of this test. The cafes have long since gone, but I know enough people scattered about the West Country to obtain the necessary cuppa and fag at 20- to 30-mile intervals, and the area is full of those A and B roads. The owner would have taken care of maintenance during the week, leaving a weekend free from mechanical problems, and this excused Enfield's failure to equip the GT with a toolbox or a reserve position on the fuel tap. Having been assured by the owner that all trivial details sich as oil in the gearbox, had been taken care of, I thus set off in the appropriate state of mind, looking for adventure, my only tool being a keyring screwdriver required to turn the ignition on.

The funniest thing about this not-entirely-serious motorcycle occurred to me shortly after I started riding it. Astonishing though it is, bearing in mind its unlikely breeding and artificially inspired conception, the Continental GT actually works. After the weekend I felt as though I'd had a really fine time and, assuming good weather I'd look forward to repeating the dose. I was frequently excited by it, and occasionally frightened. The GT is not only a cafe racer, it's in the mainstream of cafe racer tradition. For the first time since I started testing bikes I found myself remembering old experiences; 'Jesus! This is just like the old BSA, or was it the Bullet?' Behaving like a juvenile delinquent (as they were called then) is fairly normal to me, but this bike really took me back.

The key to this success is undoubtedly its handling. It runs deep into corners just like a real bike should, the frame being perfectly dead but not quite rigid. The

The Beart inspired cooling rings don't actually aid performance of the already good front brake but look neat.

steering combines high speed stability with light and precise control. It's hard to say it, but I doubt if the basic geometry could be improved. On the test bike such quality is offset, just as it was on the originals, by oversprung and underdamped rear suspension and those undamped forks. The result is totally realistic: it's possible to get either wheel hopping about, or alternatively make both leave the ground at a moment's notice. Therefore cornering speeds are limited by wheel control rather than tyre adhesion. This makes for exciting but fairly safe riding, and the sensation will be familiar to anyone who found himself branded a 'rocker' during the early sixties. Adding to the safety is a remarkably good front brake. Despite the 'cooling' discs, it's just the same old 7in unit that Enfield fitted to everything else, but this bike only weighs 300lb and stopping distances are established once again by wheel control. The forks feel as though they are about to collapse, which means that the classic accident situation — front wheel on the limits of adhesion and already running wide, and insufficient power or will to screw the back round while going into a turn — can be avoided. There's enough leeway to allow you to haul the plot upright, slow it down, and throw it back into the corner, but at the same time the operation is sufficiently hairy that you reserve it for real emergencies. In what we may call normal use, the brakes are just right for that steadying touch as the bike is pointed at the apex of a turn.

It's when it comes to the squirt part of the operation that things go a little awry. While turning out 26 horses at 7,500rpm, the GT motor in true Enfield tradition also has a very useful amount of torque. Urge is in fact increasingly available without any marked steps from around 4,000rpm right up to the bloodline, and the bike is fitted with that excellent Enfield rear hub cush drive, so delivery is always smooth —

Clip-on handlebars, flyscreen, modified casquette and, of course, the fibreglass tank make the GT a junior Boy Racer.

Powerful enough to provide an interesting time for novices the Continental GT was an excellent tool for learning on.

perhaps too smooth. No doubt I'm being a little unfair to a 250, but I did miss that feeling coming out of corners when the front end goes light and skittery (remember the undamped forks) and the back, helped by hard springs, chops about under the input of raw power. It has to be said that I enjoyed going into corners rather than coming out of them. At the top end of the speed range, a reasonable 70 to 80mph, the motor is in fact responsive enough for the throttle alone to be used for setting the bike up for a curve, but modern roads are really too much for it and the GT's real home is still the random twists of country B roads. In this sort of territory, it's just right, running at around 50 to 60, making noises that you can easily pretend are coming from a big hot old single. On such roads there's something happening all the time, braking, acceleration, gear-changing, going for the last bit of power, taking advantage of all the usable space. At such times it's possible to forget how crippl-ingly uncomfortable the riding position is, that the GT is only a 250 with pushrods, and that out there it's also 1980.

The bike's major failing was the gearbox. If the five-speed unit was worse than this four-speeder I can see the necessity for the spare cluster that went with the GT. Even at a standstill with the engine stopped and making selection by hand, neutral is difficult to find. This is probably because it floats about the gearbox

Steering, suspension and a stiff frame encourage the rider to look for those twisty backroads for maximum pleasure.

and hides between other gears, usually second and third on the way down. I ended up finding roads which required only third and fourth, the two gears which were always there. Even the third to fourth change was irritatingly slow when all the revs were being used, and I eventually had to accept it as a limitation on performance. At least it's not the only cafe racer I've had gearbox problems with!

Naturally I also ran out of petrol, not once but twice. On the first occasion it was because I'd forgotten that manufacturers' fuel tank capacity figures are always optimistic, and on the second occasion because I was having too much fun to notice how many miles I'd done. The patron saint of road testers did me proud both times (thanks Pete), and it is reasonable to assume that similar good fortune might have attended the crazed youths who were supposed to buy this bike. I even had to borrow a screwdriver, to tighten up the chainguard, just like it used to happen in the old days.

Final confirmation that the GT was and is a real cafe racer came from the reaction of the spectators. In its day this style of machine was universally damned, in the same way as the much more innocuous 'sixteener' mopeds of today are condemned. The cafe racer's only adherents wre the owners and the teenaged wenches who found it all heroic (dammit, some of it *was* heroic). Riding the GT now I found dogs barking, cars hooting, and people standing in their front gardens scowling. Every policeman I passed fixed it with a careful scrutiny, and in every small village I could sense people feeling terrorised. Flicking round a country corner, feeling like Angel Nieto or some other real racer, I became aware of two girls sitting on a fence, their gazes fixed on this noisy apparition, mouths open slightly, expressions sending messages that could have got us all into lots of trouble. And I remembered, yes folks, it was just like this. Learning to ride properly, being frightened but not hurt when it was done badly, being rewarded by the bike's response when it was done well, being excited, making lots of noise, going too fast. Were it not for the fact that this is still possible, with better bikes — with *this* bike — I'd have to say, 'Those were the days'.

Of course it's well known that I'm a proponent of working bikes, given to recommending all kinds of modifications intended to provide greater reliability and better cost effectiveness. What then could be the most appropriate function for the GT, apart from the extravagant and socially dubious fun? Given its riding position, which you have to experience to even imagine, the lack of the most rudimentary luggage or tool space, the noise, the reserve-less tank, what possible use can it have? Its owner, who admits to being technically illiterate and runs the best disco in Bristol, uses it for the task most perfectly suited to Royal Enfields everywhere; he drives it to work.

Specification

250cc ROYAL ENFIELD CONTINENTAL GT

ENGINE

Type	**ohv single**
Bore x stroke	**70 x 64.5mm**
Capacity	**248cc**
Compression ratio	**9.5:1**
Carburation	**Amal Concentric**
Bhp @ rpm	**26 @ 7,500**
Primary drive	**single-row chain**
Clutch	**wet, multi-plate**
Gearbox	**5 speed (see text)**
Electrical system	**12v. 120w alternator, battery and coil ignition**

DIMENSIONS

Wheelbase	**52in**
Seat height	**29.5in**
Ground clearance	**5.5in**
Dry weight	**300lb**
Fuel capacity	**3½gal**
Tyres	
(front)	**3.25 x 17 Avon SM**
(rear)	**3.25 x 17 Avon SM**
Brakes	
(front)	**7in sls**
(rear)	**6in sls**

PERFORMANCE

Top speed	**80-85mph (claimed)**
Standing ¼ mile	**19 sec (est)**
Fuel consumption	**58.5mpg**

750cc Royal Enfield Interceptor Series 2

by Royce Creasey

Royal Enfield Interceptor

Reading this article, maybe just looking at the pictures, you'll notice that there's a subtle difference in approach between this Royal Enfield Series II Interceptor and most classic machines. This one wasn't found in a ditch and lovingly restored over a period of some years. Neither is it in the hands of an enthusiastic collector of late Enfield twins. Like huge numbers of other English bikes, it works. It gets left out at night, and used when and where it's needed.

I get the distinct impression that if it stopped working it could find itself in the hands of a collector pretty smartly. Its main claim to fame is as an example of virtually the last thoughts of the Royal Enfield motorcycle company. That means there's a lot of development behind this bike, so much so that it could be considered the last of the many. The Norton front forks, wheel and brake are standard, although the Tickle twin-leading-shoe back-plate is an addition. Just under the swinging arm nuts are the nuts that clamp the alloy block. The oil filter on the front of the engine is non-standard; in fact it's a Norton Commando unit, and replaces the strange oil cooler that Enfield fitted from 1970 onwards.

This bike belongs to Jeff Lewis, one of the L & D Motors family who effectively are Royal Enfield in the South West, and was built up from parts returned to the old Enfield service department under guarantee. As you can imagine, this reversed pattern of selective assembly has led to a few problems in the past, and Jeff still reckons there's some way to go before everything is pulling together. This sorting-out process seems inevitable with built-up bikes, and can last years. In addition to the non-standard brake and oil filter, purists will also note minor differences in the way Jeff and Royal Enfield arranged the headstock, and then of course there's the tank. Ah yes, I was saving the tank. You didn't think Royal Enfield would ever get it on to fit a snappy number like that to a road bike, did you? Right. I'm told that this is the one and only racing tank off the one and only works production racer that Royal Enfield put together and raced a couple of times in 1969. Gosh, how about that! I've always thought that Royal Enfield tanks were pretty horrible, so it's comforting to know that the race shop thought so, too. Apparently the rest of the proddy racer is also still running about somewhere, probably pulling a chair full of plumbing.

The Series II Interceptor differs considerably from all the earlier Enfield twins. For a start it's considerably slower than the Series I. In this respect it's just like the Triumph Bonneville, which seems to run slower the newer it gets. Sometimes I think there must have been a time warp operating back in the fifties and sixties that allowed bikes to reach higher speeds! Apart from the frame tweaks mentioned so far there is also a longer swinging arm on the Series II with a bracing cross-tube, but the biggest difference is in the engine. The remarkable three-pump Enfield lubrication system with all those filters and bungs, that was used on just about every engine they made since the beginning, was dumped in favour of a single pump wet-sump car-like system running at a convincing 60psi. This required different and impressively massive casings, and the gearbox casing got smoothed in a bit at the same time. Big-ends are conventional shell type, with a huge ball main on the drive side and a roller bearing on the timing side: Enfield always did have slightly odd ideas about main bearings.

At the top end, Amal Concentrics replace Monoblocs with the usual benefits, but it seems possible that the cam is the reason for the lower speed of the Series II. Primary drive follows normal Enfield practice until you notice the splined clutch. It's a really solid number that replaces that dreadful dog-eared thing they used to fit, and Enfield owners everywhere may be pleased to know that it fits all models down to the Bullet. Inside the gearbox, things are exactly as Albion intended all those years ago. The gears themselves are a bit wider than in earlier versions to cope with the power increases gained in the last three or four decades, but this is still a vintage box, even the Velocette change feels smooth by comparison. When I think about that Enfield gearchange, cliches like "very positive" spring to mind, but actually it's like breaking off a $\frac{3}{8}$in bolt with a big lever. And all the gears are undercut, so there's no question of changing anything unless the power is eased right off the transmission. As for finding neutral at a standstill, there's a neutral selector that you stamp on that works (if you're not in bottom) sometimes. Otherwise it's a case of just sitting there holding the clutch lever in and being surprised that this is an English clutch that takes that sort of treatment without drag, subsequent slip or any change in adjustment. That is probably the biggest single improvement Royal Enfield ever made.

How, you may ask, do I have this casual understanding of the innards of the Series II Interceptor? Well, for reasons I'm much too polite to talk about I found myself travelling down some local road at around 65mph when three components inside the gearbox that were designed to rotate as three suddenly and doggedly decided to move as one. My main preoccupation after this gearbox lock-up was the rate at which the resultant fish-tailing would get rough enough to dump me in front of a following car, but I was also aware of the ease with

Redesigned oil pump gives the timing side a new look but the rest of the motor is very similar to the earliest Meteor. The Albion gearbox is completely unchanged.

which the bike could be controlled with only one wheel rotating. This state of tension was equally abruptly broken when the chain fortuitously snapped, allowing me to free-wheel to a safe if rather lucky halt. The chain was even polite enough to park itself on top of the gearbox while I coasted downhill to a convenient phone.

I remember at the time being aware of the difficulties of testing a bike owned by a friend who is also the sole supplier of my Velo and Enfield spares. Had it been the new Tobitsu XBY 1500 V8 on test I could have just let it collapse onto the verge and terminated the test with a brief phone call to the importer: *"Yeah, it's by the road out of Flax Bourton somewhere — Yeah, the keys are in it — No, I dunno what went wrong, see yer"*. Slam, click. Reality being what it is, and with the *Classic Bike* photo team due to turn up the next day, there was nothing for it but to resurrect long-disused skills in massaging transmissions and hurl it all back together again. Using L & D's workshop, it was a real pleasure to have any part I could think of immediately to hand. A running Interceptor coincided with the arrival of the cameras, and it was time to get back to actually riding the beast again.

When they first appeared, the 700cc Constellation and the 750cc Interceptor (which was instantly dubbed the 'Contraceptive') were definitely in the heavy metal league. But this particular Enfield was a surprise. The first time I climbed over the high (31in) seat and pushed away the prop stand it seemed much lighter than I had expected — there's just got to be a lot of empty space inside all that massiveness. In fact it's fairly heavy by English standards, at around 450lb, but it just doesn't feel it.

The next revelation was the steering. The Roadholder forks behave just as they do on the front of a Dominator: very light and very precise. At first the front end felt so light that I was sure that if I hit a bump the bike would snap straight into a vicious judder, but it turned out to be quite

Dropping the famous casquette gives this Enfield an updated – if idiosyncratic – appearance.

dead at all the speeds I got up to. What Enfield achieved was a successful marriage between a firm but less than solid frame with a low natural frequency, and those excellent forks. Neither end gets the other going, resulting in the comfort of a late Triumph and the precision steering of a Dominator.

Encouraged by this discovery, I set out for the nearest bit of nice country road to see what it was like on the footrests. It turned out to be a centre-stand grinder, but you hear the graunching well before there's any shortage of adhesion, so naturally you hang off the seat some to keep the bike upright and then it really is rather good. The front end can be steered really well so it's possible to push the Interceptor hard enough to get it drifting, and then the motor produces all this stomp right on demand which brings it all back into line: very controllable and lots of fun, except that it all required a bit more climbing about than I'm used to. The Girling struts at the rear were exhibiting the usual syndrome (great while they last) and the front forks could have done with some bushes, but the pitching from the rear end under power changes and the squirm under braking from the front end didn't cause any problems in control, it just looked untidy.

The biggest disappointment at this point was the motor's inability to roll-on during gearchanges. I've always liked the heavy flywheels found in the English singles and some modern bikes (the Laverda Jota for one) and the engine characteristics they produce. Closing the throttle for a gear change only takes the load off the transmission, while the flywheels serve to maintain engine speed. The Interceptor motor is almost Japanese in the way that it slows down as soon as the throttle is closed, and this made fast 'A' road work something of an effort. In fact during the whole test I never really got it flowing down 'A' roads the way I like. This is a fault shared by all the parallel twins to some extent — like most two-strokes they just don't like cruising at much above 70. At lower, country touring speeds the engine feels much more pleasant. Between 3,000 and 4,000rpm it's very smooth, and surprisingly powerful in terms of sudden stomp. At this sort of rate though, I would have preferred more stability in the steering. The front never went anywhere it wasn't pointed, but it did need pointing.

On the whole I wasn't over-impressed by the Interceptor's out-of-town performance. In fact its nicest performance envelope is in the same league as that of the Velocette MSS, the Enfield coming out ahead on exciting scratch-ability, but not by much. As a long distance fast tourer it could well be a real pain unless a route could be chosen that kept speeds down. Then, snarling out of hairpins, going light over humpback bridges, it sure is fun,

John Tickle backplate is not standard equipment but the Norton Roadholder forks are, to the handling's benefit.

for as long as the rider's got the strength left to climb about on it.

The Interceptor's power delivery consists largely of torque. I've always thought of the Bullet as 'son of stump-puller', but if that is so then this model has to be ole' man stump-puller himself. Rolling at about five miles an hour in first with the clutch home, a handful of throttle smoothly heaves the front end off the ground while the motor just grunts a bit harder. Hanging onto fourth out in the country from about 1,000rpm results in a steady increase in speed until about 3,500 when it gets almost dizzying until around 5,000rpm, beyond which point the motor seems to lose interest. It's supposed to go to 7,000, and looking at the twin carbs I'm surprised it isn't more revvy. The cam is almost certainly responsible for this effect, so perhaps a Series I unit would transform the performance.

The 'one gear at a time' acceleration, the huge torque off the bottom end and the precise steering actually point to a use where this is a very good bike: it's a hot commuter. Any good bike can be

Royal Enfield Interceptor

hustled through traffic jams, the Enfield just makes it easy. At walking pace the motor will chuff over, ready to pick up at a moment's notice, and the very good lock encourages easy feet-up right-angled turns. It's a sort of urban trials bike. The useful Enfield rear cush hub is backed up by another shock absorber in the clutch, resulting in possibly the most flexible transmission ever. It's quite possible to get surge either way with sudden throttle movements, but it never gets through to the rear wheel. The big advantage is that really rude amounts of throttle can be snapped on from tick-over, yet the bike rushes forward without emitting any snatch or nasty grating feelings. The sensation is a bit strange when stopping, though. Doing the thing with the foot hitting the ground as the bike stops, man and motorcycle neatly balanced, is all very well, but next the whole machine gets dragged backwards as the rear hub unwinds. It's a quirk you get used to in time.

A major disadvantage of the Interceptor is fuel consumption, which worked out at 32mpg on this test. The bike also displayed a thirst for oil at the rate of 200mpp. Talking of oil, you may have noticed that I haven't mentioned oil leaks yet. I'm trying to think of a way of being polite about the subject, but basically if the test bike doesn't get fixed soon Jeff will probably be busted for causing an environmental hazard. It's possible to get any Enfield absolutely oil-tight, but the job is more of a challenge on the Series II Interceptor. You may also wonder why Jeff likes commuting on his bike so much when the fuel consumption alone makes this kind of use a dubious proposition. Basically, I think it's because the Interceptor makes going to work enough fun to justify the extra expense. It's not really frightening, perfectly controllable in the wet, and is equally happy being driven very slowly or quite fast. It also has the prime advantage of making a noise like Tyrannosaurus Rex pondering breakfast.

Mention of exhaust notes leads me to point out another area where the Interceptor is a real star. One of the more pleasant forms of motorcycling consists of just grooving around town late at night. It must be something to do with all those empty roads and the neon lights. At the sort of quasi-legal speeds at which such riding is done, the Interceptor is beautifully relaxed — the straights are too short for parallel twin tenseness to show. There's often the odd bit of excitement when someone doing the same thing turns up, but the Enfield looks so butch that it gives you the option

Slightly ponderous for really fast bend swinging the Interceptor Series 2 is nevertheless an exciting bike to ride hard. The steering is light and precise, the forks well damped.

of choosing to race or not. If you decide not to, a bunch of throttle has the front wheel surging off the ground and the engine growl turns into thunder. This convinces any would-be racer that the device is actually desperately fast, and they'd better not mess with it on a 380 Suzuki. Maybe I'm getting old, but when it comes to going demonically fast in confined spaces I much prefer the lighter Velocette. The Interceptor is just too much of a rocket ship in these circumstances. With rebuilt forks and another set of Girlings it might develop the necessary handling precision, but I suspect that like the other big twins, there's just a bit too much of everything to turn it loose in urban areas. Bearing in mind the newness of certain components on the test bike I was moderate in attempts at ultimate speed, although it should make it past the ton when fully run-in. But grooving round town is still where it's nicest, where the machinery intrudes least, the noise is most pleasant, and the ride most comfortable. The Joe Lucas 12-volt electrical system scores zero for design elegance, but finally gives bright, reliable lights to the British. If the bike were mine I'd fit a dimmer for riding in town, though — it's embarrassing to be that visible. Meanwhile it should be noted that the bike's owner is one of these Nordic giant types, whereas I'm some sort of dwarf, so it may be that he finds the Interceptor much easier to hurl about than I did.

Talking to Jeff after all this excitement, I got another surprise when we started to discuss main component life. As you'd expect, the rear tyre and chain are good for about 10,000 miles, while the primary chain, well protected against anything as crude as road shock by all that rubber, hasn't managed to wear out yet. The bottom end is showing signs of lasting about 20,000 miles at a time, however. Considering the apparently excellent lubrication system this is rather a short period, although crankshaft life will possibly increase as better parts are selected and the art of assembling big Enfield twins is fully learned.

High bore wear, all too common with the long piston strokes used in most parallel twins, is probably an incurable problem, although a big air filter would help. Various solutions to some of the other problems that Enfield left behind come to mind, but given the use that this particular bike is put to and the limitations inherent in its layout, it's probably not worth refining it further. I find it difficult to justify the high fuel consumption and the huge engine in terms of the performance usefully available. I think it could be made to go very fast indeed, but then I'm not sure it would be reliable at higher speeds. As it is, the Interceptor is reliable, easy to work on, really nice to ride in traffic and down summer lanes at the sort of speeds that keep you awake but allow you to read the road signs.

Specification

750cc ROYAL ENFIELD INTERCEPTOR SERIES 2

ENGINE

Type	ohv parallel twin
Bore x stroke	71 x 93mm
Capacity	736cc
Compression ratio	8.5:1
Carburation	2 x 30mm Amal Concentrics
Bhp @ rpm	55 @ 6500
Primary drive	duplex chain
Clutch	multiplate, wet
Gearbox	4 speed
Electrical system	120w 12v Lucas alternator, coil ignition
Lighting	50/55w halogen headlamp

DIMENSIONS

Wheelbase	57in
Seat height	31in
Ground clearance	5.75in
Kerb weight	426lb
Fuel capacity	3½gal
Tyres	
(front)	4.10 x 19 Avon Roadrunner
(rear)	4.25 x 18 Avon Roadrunner
Brakes	
(front)	8in, twin leading shoe
(rear)	7in, single leading shoe

PERFORMANCE

Top speed	105mph (est)
Standing ¼ mile	14.5secs (est)
Fuel consumption	32mpg
Braking distance from 30mph	30ft (approx)
Owner	Jeff Lewis, L & D Motors, Bristol.

1936 500cc Rudge Ulster

by Ted Davis

Rudge Ulster

Ulster is to Rudge what Manx is to Norton. As the winners of the famous Irish classic on more than one occasion during the thirties, it really meant something when Rudge applied the name of the race to their top-of-the-range model.

The Ulster was launched in 1929 and remained in production until 1939, when the company ceased to manufacture motorcycles. This was a great loss, as for many years the factory had enjoyed a reputation for innovative engineering. An infinitely variable transmission, four-valve cylinder heads, a linked braking system and even, as long ago as 1929, a five-speed gearbox were among the radical developments tried by Rudge. Some of these features are still being hailed as bold and exciting today, with Moto Guzzi making much of their excellent linked braking arrangement, and the Japanese getting into a lather of excitement over their latterday excursion into four-valve heads for road machines.

Not only were Rudge unafraid to experiment, but in their time they were successful as mass producers. During the 39 years of the company's life output rose to many thousands of units per annum, and at one time 7,000 bicycles a week were being made. Yet, like Sunbeam and Vincent, they used the minimum of bought-out parts, the bulk of their machines being designed and manufactured in-plant.

The Ulster was a well-made, good-looking motorcycle, equipped with the ever-impressive 8in Miller headlamp, and finished in the inevitable black and gold. It was really the huge coupled brakes, the four-valve cylinder head and the twin exhaust pipes matched with above average performance — 90-plus mph and 60-plus mpg — that made the machine stand out as a classic in its own time. Rudge engineering and quality were superior to most other marques, while reliability was equal to similarly priced 500s. The price itself was definitely up-market, and only a handful of exotic bikes cost more. In 1939, for example, when an Ulster went for £82, a BSA Gold Star was listed at 50p (or ten bob, if you prefer) more.

I'm in the fortunate position of being able to go back over forty years to recall just how good the Ulster was in its day. In the spring of 1939 I felt distinctly apprehensive when I took delivery of a low-mileage 1938 model, with the newly-introduced right-foot gear lever. The horrifyingly high price for this mint-condition bike was £57 50p, and my concern was partly due to the financial condition I had been forced into to raise this amount (so much for the good old days).

I was no stranger to the model, as I had been using an old speedway version on the grass in '38, and had therefore acquired a healthy respect for this potent 500. Certainly my road-going Ulster was quick and, if I remember correctly, mechanically noisy. And while it

A truly vintage layout – nuts, bolts, cables and two friction dampers, one for the girders one for the steering.

handled quite well, it wasn't in the same class as an International Norton, a Velocette, or the then very unconventional sprung-frame Vincent-HRD. The Ulster's rigid rear end hopped around quite a lot, and the rather stiff, short-travel girder forks with their encased spring and Rudge patented one-piece links compared unfavourably with the softer ride produced by the Brampton and Webb girders of the period.

On acceleration and top speed the Ulster was a match for the Inter Norton, the dashing new Triumph Speed Twin, or any other 500 of its day, and indeed the model remained quicker than many bikes produced post-war. Although huge in comparison with the brakes fitted to other makes, the 8in front unit and 7½in rear drum were little better in their stopping powers. As on modern Guzzis, operation of the foot pedal applied both brakes simultaneously, while the normal handlebar lever permitted independent application of the front brake only. But, unlike Guzzi and their use of hydraulics, Rudge had to depend on a dubious cable system.

It must be remembered that most pre-war braking systems were inferior to post-war designs, with the exception of Vincent-HRD, who employed four brakes on their machines and enjoyed the benefits of rear springing. Any attempt to achieve really good rear wheel braking with a rigid frame is doomed on all but the smoothest surfaces.

Having covered so many miles on a great variety of

Quick for its time the overhead cam unit was mechanically noisy but well made and beautifully finished.

There's nothing new about four-valve heads. The Ulster's 500cc motor gave in the region of 24bhp at 6000rpm.

old and new designs since my original experiences with Ulsters, my response to the machine today is very different to the excitement I felt back in 1939. Gone is the apprehension; after all, this is only a 500 in a world of megabikes, and it weighs less and is slower than many modern 250s.

The test bike is a 1936 semi-radial four-valver with exposed springs and bronze head, and while its level of vibration would have been taken as normal in its day, it would now be regarded as unacceptable, especially at the higher engine speeds where it intrudes most. The degree of vibration is similar to that of a Norton Inter or BSA Gold Star, and certainly excessive when compared to a post-war Velo or Vincent Comet.

The brakes, too, seem unimpressive, and the ride and handling leave much to be desired, as does the mechanical noise put out by the engine. The bike is

Not as agile as a Norton Inter or Velo, the Ulster managed very well on short-travel girders and a rigid rear end.

still a flier, however, 80mph coming up quite quickly, while acceleration compares favourably with any road-going 500cc single. I was unable to find a figure for the power output of the 1936 Ulster — Rudge seem to have taken the Rolls-Royce attitude and implied that their engines were always "adequate" in this department — but I did discover that a 1934 model gave 24bhp at 6,000rpm. As an interesting comparison, *Motor Cycle Mechanics* magazine last year tested a Yamaha SR500 single at 28bhp at the rear wheel and described this two-valve, sohc motor as "disappointingly gutless"!

The first thing you notice when mounting the Ulster is the low, 26in seat height. As you swing a leg over you clear the saddle and pillion pad by a foot, an experience very different from modern bikes, with their seat heights of thirty inches or more that came with the introduction of rear-wheel springing.

The engine usually fired after three or four lusty kicks with the air lever closed and the manual ignition lever in the retarded position (tight cable). To assist starting, the Ulster sports a half-compression lever, which is mounted on the right side of the crankcase together with a plunger to indicate oil pressure.

The clutch is light to operate and smooth on take-up, while progression through the gearbox is positive, despite the rather long lever travel. Bottom is at the top of the lever movement, while the lever itself is located on the left hand side — shades of things to come!

Handling on well-surfaced roads is smooth and positive, although fast cornering runs the risk of grinding the quite considerable mass of ironware that is mounted perilously low. The limitations of the rather stiff, short-travel front end are really shown up by bumpy roads, when comfort for a passenger on the 6 x 4in pillion pad becomes distinctly spartan. The sprung saddle helps the rider, however, and the 27in wheels also assist in ironing out the shocks and prevent the lack of rear springing from being as disastrous as it might have been.

What'll she do flat out? Sneaking a look over my shoulder and tucking my chin into the tank, I watched the needle of the Smith's speedo nudge round the dial. We made 90 on a slight downhill gradient, which was cheating a little, but that still represents a great performance from a 44-year-old bike. The sensation of speed was tremendous, and the experience reminded me that the same rate of travel on my Ducati V-twin seems like 60mph. No wonder I felt in awe of the Ulster at the impressionable age of 17!

In retrospect, one can see that the Ulster fully lived up to its name. For any enthusiast interested in running one of these bikes there is an active owners' club with a membership of around 500 and a good spares scheme. The bike's sound basic engineering makes life easier for the restorer, or the rebuilder who simply wants a good working classic, a role that many Ulsters enjoy today.

Specification

1936 500cc RUDGE ULSTER

ENGINE

Type	four-valve single
Bore x stroke	85 x 88mm
Capacity	499cc
Compression ratio	n/a
Carburation	Amal
Bhp @ rpm	n/a
Primary drive	single-row chain
Clutch	multi-plate wet
Gearbox	4 speed
Electrical system	BTH magneto, Miller dynamo

DIMENSIONS

Wheelbase	54in
Seat height	26.5in
Ground clearance	4.75in
Kerb weight	400lb
Fuel capacity	3½gal
Tyres	
(front)	3.00 x 27in
(rear)	3.25 x 27in
Brakes	
(front)	8in sls
(rear)	7.5in sls

PERFORMANCE

Top speed	88 mph (est)
Standing ¼ mile	18secs (est)
Fuel consumption	70mpg
Braking distance	
from 30mph	34ft
Owner	Bob Culver, Letchworth, Herts.

500cc Sunbeam S7 and S8

by Jerry Clayton

Sunbeam S7 and S8

Tarmac motorway stretched straight and true like some art student's exercise in perspective towards the brow of the incline some half mile ahead. Beneath the tank, the engine responded weakly to frantic throttle twisting as I sought to induce the last of the mixture through the carb. Finally it died. In the silence that followed I heard my own tones of self reproach – "No miracles this time" — for I'm usually one of the luckiest blokes under the sun in such dire circumstances. I glanced at my watch; nine minutes past six. Twenty minutes had elapsed since I'd collected the 1954 S7 from arch-enthusiast Tony Wilkins at Honda dealers Ken Ives of Leicester.

When I next checked on the time, it was fifteen minutes past six on that July evening and I was sitting safely in the back of a Toyota Hiace, driven by two very kind Japanese Nova Formula Three race mechanics, and clutching the handlebar of the Sunbeam as it rested somewhat haphazardly on its propstand.

At Watford Gap services the Sunbeam and I disembarked, and my saviours ran circles around the bike chatting excitedly and clicking away with the inevitable camera. Such are the mysteries of the Orient, they were attending the British car Grand Prix at Brands the following weekend, but in their inscrutable fashion had decided to stay at Silverstone! Ah so.

And come to think of it, there's a certain amount of intrigue attached to the Sunbeam S7 (and later the sportier S8), which was the first truly fresh British design to emerge from the post-war era. Despite having only 4½ inches of ground clearance and a fuel consumption regarded to be on the high side for the day, September 1956 saw a decade pass and the announcement of 'no change' for the balloon-tyred twin. To some degree, at least, the Sunbeam had proved a success against the odds.

To recapture more fully the thinking behind this wet sump, in-line, unit construction, overhead camshaft, shaft driven twin, it's not a bad scheme to trace back through Sunbeam's history.

In the late nineteenth century, John Marston and Co of Wolverhampton were knocking out saucepans and odds and sods. The coming of the bicycle changed all that, and in 1890 the company switched production to the new form of self-propelled transport. Inevitably, their first motorcycle was produced – a 350cc side-valve – in 1912. Finished in green and silver and of first rate quality, it commanded a high retail figure. But few were sold, and Marston and Co appear to have never appreciated the sad fact that high quality and high price were the underlying reasons for their lack of real marketing success.

Bristling with advanced features the S7 has acquired a reputation as a 'gentleman's machine' – as intended.

Power unit and driveline of the later S8 were virtually identical to those of the S7.

Design includes a car type sump, making big end replacement easy, and the pancake dynamo.

In 1937 Marston and Co were taken over by Associated Motor Cycles, and the existing range of 250, 350, 500 and 600cc models persevered to the outbreak of war. During hostilities, in 1943, the Sunbeam name changed hands again – this time to BSA. Crazy? Well no, not really, for BSA had a new design up their sleeve ready to launch on the post-war world. Always regarded as being 'the gentleman's motorcycle', the name Sunbeam suited the BSA directors to a fine degree. The bike they had on the stocks was just what the Sunbeam tag implied.

The man behind the S7 (does any employee know why that designation was chosen?) announced in spring 1946 was Erling Poppe. Originally a motorcycle designer, Poppe's energies had been largely channelled, prior to this project, into automobile work. So perhaps it was inevitable that a high degree of fresh thinking – as far as motorcycles were concerned – would manifest itself in his new two-wheeled project, and it can all be traced back very easily from the S7. Wet sump lubrication, plain bearings, overhead cam aluminium in-line engine, a car type clutch, shaft drive and those distinctive 4.50 x 16 and 4.75 x 16 front and rear tyres became the distinctive hallmarks of the new 'Beam'. The wheels were interchangeable, the frame fully sprung, and the electrics (which included coil ignition) carefully tucked out of harm's way. The bike was finished at first in black, with alloy and chromium contrasts, but the colour switched in March 1949 to Mist Green and compares in some way with Marston's own first motorcycle back in 1912. Cost came into it too, for to own the new Sunbeam you had to pay £70 more than for BSA's comparable orthodox 500cc twin, the A7 (a model number which may or may not explain that Sunbeam marking).

The quietness of the all-alloy engine with its over-square 70mm bore x 63.5mm stoke was, and is, amazing and both the revs and power output claimed (25bhp at 5,800rpm) belie the slightly rorty purr of the exhaust. Just why Poppe opted to use the underslung hardened steel worm gear running on a phosphor bronze wheel remains a mystery. In automobile terms it was as dead a practice as chain drive being superseded by crown-wheel and pinion bevels and spiral bevels, and would never be able to take much more than the Sunbeam's claimed output. Even so, the unit rarely gives trouble provided it is supplied with the correct lubricant, but the handbook warns against becoming alarmed at the first sighting of yellowish bronze particles in the oil during routine changes — this is apparently perfectly normal. And bear in mind too, that the Sunbeam was also designed for sidecar work with 5:22 worm and drive alternatives to the standard 6:23 arrangement. Sunbeam produced a very neat little sidecar, colour-matched to suit the bikes,

And while Tony Wilkins is enthusiastic about all his bikes, in all probability he wouldn't claim to be a marque specialist on the two 'Beams' he owns — the S7 tested here and the S8 we rode for a day before the nipple popped off the clutch cable. The man most deserving of that title is Bob Stewart, of Stewart Engineering in Disraeli Road, Putney.

The clutch on the test S7 was well clapped, with the lever slack to the tune of about an inch at the handlebar. Tony and I, in our ignorance and perhaps egged on somewhat by the collapse of the S8 item, decided that the clutch cable had passed the realms of usefulness. "If you do go to Stewart Engineering for more info, ask them if they've got a clutch cable," Tony yelled as I headed south. In Putney another tale unfolded.

Oh sure, apart from tank badges Bob Stewart's got everything you need — *everything* — and at very reasonable prices, too. He became interested in the bikes when he met his wife-to-be — she rode one — and the whole Sunbeam side of his business took off from there. As Mist Green as the S7 smoking in the gutter outside, I ventured to ask for the cable.

After listening to my explanation of the symptoms, Bob took a look. "Clutch thrust bearing's packing up — must be unpleasant changing gear. Good lord, this rear lower rubber mounting for the engine has had it and someone has straightened out the high frequency vibration damper under the rear of the tank. The engine's shifted forwards about half an inch. Have you felt any clonking? That's the engine hitting the lower frame tube and..."

And from there we started to learn a whole new ball game, because that's the only way to describe the business of owning a Sunbeam. But the enthusiasm of Stewart and his team has to be seen. A bike like Tony's you can buy for anything between £250 and £400, depending on condition. Then you start to sort it out with parts from Stewart Engineering. Or you can take advantage of their rebuild service; it's painstaking to a degree and the cost of refurbishing a bike brought in by a customer averages around the £1000 mark. If the job costs less, however, the savings *are* passed on to the customer. An S7 they were fettling in the workshop had been quoted at £900, but was working out at less than that figure.

Because the engine is oversquare, it gives the distinct impression of being buzzy. Nearly all the way down the M1, the S7 had stuck at 70mph. There were traces of oil appearing from the cambox, and it appears that 65mph is probably the optimum speed for sustained touring without causing duress. Yet because the oil pump is highly efficient, such occurences are far from rare. Indeed, the pistons of the S7 and S8 were fitted with an additional oil scraper ring. The two compression rings occupied their usual position in lands at the top of the piston with the standard scraper just a little lower — normal motorcycle practice. But below the gudgeon pin there is a further oil scraper ring to clear excess oil from the cylinder bores on each downward stroke.

The bike has coil ignition with a car type distributor driven from the cam chain immediately behind the cylinders. It's a component that can cause a few problems on both the S7 and S8 as the auto/advance units wear. But have no fear, for Bob Stewart has the answer, although you'll probably have to leave the unit with him for a day or so.

It's now a fairly expensive investment for a company like Stewart Engineering to maintain a stock of parts. For instance, GKN insisted on a minimum run for the bonded drive/gearbox couplings, and this cost Bob just under £8000! Ironically, it's a part that wears well. Looking at the test S7, Bob reckoned that the unit needed replacing, but added that the item on the bike was probably the original.

The S7 and its balloon tyres became part of the

Final drive was a weak point, the underslung wormdrive limiting power output of the potentially quick motor.

Balloon tyres, interchangeable front and rear at the twist of a tommy bar, distinguish the earlier touring model.

The later, sporty S8, however, used the front forks, brake and wheel from BSA's A7. The deep mudguards remained the same.

motorcycling scene during the late forties, through the fifties and into the sixties — despite production coming to a halt in 1957. Like earlier Sunbeams it was still 'a gentleman's motorcycle' — a two-wheeled car almost, with a dipstick on the left of the crankcase for checking the sump oil, all the electrics hidden behind a panel on the right, and the battery — 6-volt — tucked away behind a similar arrangement on the left. Finally, there was that unusual choice of worm gear and wheel final drive.

BSA, however, had done their homework quite well. The bike had been thoroughly tested immediately after the war, and they'd even breathed heavily on the engine to get almost 95mph. Handling proved suspect, however, probably due as much as anything to the strange front fork arrangement fitted to earlier models. These were, as the handbooks of the era described them, 'extremely substantial'. The legs were widely spaced and acted merely as sliders. Located centrally behind the sliders was a large spring fixed at the top to the top yoke and at its lower end to a bridge spanning the two sliders and retaining the mudguard. A smaller rebound spring was used, and the whole was totally enclosed and lubricated by grease gun. The sliders, on the other hand, featured phosphor bronze bushing lubricated by two oil soaked wicks made of cotton with oil reservoir cups above, which required attention only after very long periods. The arrangement was dropped after two years of production in favour of what we now consider to be more orthodox forks with oil damping. At the same time, with the advent of the S8 model, the S7 with new forks became the S7 De Luxe. Every variant had plunger rear suspension.

The S8 version appeared in March 1949, with its main difference being the lighter, more orthodox mudguards, wheels and brakes, a cast alloy silencer and a compression ratio upped from the S7's original 6.5:1 to 7.2:1. Poppe's original reversed handlebar levers — vintage fashion with the cables enclosed in the 'bar — had been dropped on the S7 almost immediately, so these were in fact no longer a feature. But the S8 retained the enclosed electrics, battery and the neat little toolbox down behind the engine on the left hand side. The strange thing about the S8 and its sportier outlook was that it suddenly seemed to uprate the renamed S7 De Luxe as well.

The S8 featured loose liners in the cylinder block instead of the pressed-fit alloy iron liners formerly used. The S7 followed suit. Then the compression ratio of the export S7 was uprated just a shade to 6.8:1 and new camshafts fitted for home and export markets. At this stage, there was no revision of valve timing despite the new shaft, but in 1950 the timing was considerably revised. Valves opened earlier and closed later, probably as the direct result of a change in ideas over the benefits of slower opening ramp cams.

The influence of the S8 makes itself apparent on every S7 manufactured after May 27 1949. These were now the S7 De Luxe, and all the engines carried the prefix S8 (the test bike was S8—13674), while the frame number started with the prefix S7. It's an easy way to tell a De Luxe from a standard S7, although the lack of the central spring unit on the front forks will indicate the same thing. The revised valve timing altered little in the way of performance. If anything, it probably had the effect of making an already quiet engine a shade more silent.

The S8 retained the aluminium covers over the spark plugs and also carried an air cleaner. It arrived on the scene on March 25 1949, and two months later the S7 De Luxe followed suit with the air cleaner instead of a strangler choke cover arrangement. The cantilevered pan saddle with its suspension spring running down inside the frame tube was dropped on the S8, which instead featured a standard tri-point spring-fixing saddle of the era. On Tony Wilkins' S8 the forward fixing for the front spring had undergone some minor butchery, but even so the seat was still surprisingly comfortable.

While the S7 De Luxe retained its character and its 4½ inches of ground clearance with those 4.50 x 16 and 4.75 x 16 balloon tyres, the lighter S8 offered increased ground clearance to 5½ inches with standard 3.25 x 19 and 4.00 x 18 wheels and covers. Strangely, while mentioning tyres, some early 1948 and all the '47 S7s were fitted with a 4.75 front tyre of studded pattern — that *must* have been fun!

The fulcrum adjusted eight-inch brakes of the S7 reminded me of those original Marston saucepans — or at least the front one did. The wheels of this model are interchangeable — a feature lost on the S8 which also carried a 500cc BSA A7 front fork. The test bike had a slightly oval front brake, and this accounts for a stopping figure from 30mph at around the 36ft mark, which isn't bad considering that it was improved by only three or four feet when everything was set up correctly.

More vibration than would be normal made its way through to the rider, not only because the engine appeared to have shifted forward slightly and the aforementioned rubbers were worn, but the clearance between the lower downtube forward snubbers (normally set at between 15 and 20 thou) was way out, allowing the engine to rock laterally quite loosely.

Even in this condition, however, the Sunbeam

The lighter S8 has an inch more ground clearance than the S7 but both machines offer a safe, comfortable ride.

showed signs of commendable perseverance and at night, despite the electrical system being only six volt, the eight-inch headlight provided a tremendous spread of light to the extent that it had to be pushed downwards slightly to avoid causing annoyance to oncoming road users. There are green and red 'idiot' lights set in the headlamp shell — the green being for oil pressure and the red for dynamo output. If both are functioning the lights extinguish when the engine is started. Again, it's typical car stuff and very unusual for this era of motorcycling. It's a simple bike to start via the normally located kickstart — so positioned thanks to skew gears — a lazy kick being enough to set the engine burbling into life.

Fuel consumption averaged out over the entire test at a shade over 66mpg and the highest practical top speed to be recorded was 70mph, although the speedometer needle would rise to 78mph on long downhill runs.

And in spite of the wear and tear, the clonking gear-change and sloppy engine mounts, the bike was still eminently comfortable — but not so for a passenger, who seemed as if she went up on her seat when the bike hit a bump at the same time as the rider's seat threatened to disappear down the frame tube! A dual seat, according to Bob Stewart, is the answer.

Despite the lack of ground clearance I really enjoyed riding the two bikes. The S7 may be elephantine, but the only serious restriction is that of ground clearance, and the bike must surely rank as a classic if only for all the original thought that went into it. While being more practical, the S8 tended, for my money at least, to make just too many concessions to conventional motorcycle practices of the period. This was probably for economic reasons — penny pinching if you like — although the factory attempted to disguise such motives by calling it a sporting mount. Typical of the economies is the tinny looking seven-inch front brake with standard cable take-up, while the S7 and S7 De Luxe featured adjustable fulcrums as on a car.

I have memories of watching a Mist Green Sunbeam S7 and matching sidecar following our motor coach (charabancs as they once called them) as it returned down the Eastbourne Road one wet summer's evening many years ago. The driver wore a long fawn riding coat, and a cheesecutter cap with goggles and would wave at us kids as we pressed our noses against the steamy back window. Now one of those combos I would dearly love to ride — the guy looked so pleased with his lot even in that weather!

Sincere thanks to Tony Wilkins for the loan of his S7 De Luxe — I think we both learnt a lot. Bob Stewart is also chairman of The Sunbeam Fellowship, but membership enquiries should be sent to Mrs Jo Tompolska, at 55 Bective Road, Putney, London SW15. Membership entitles you to copies of the Fellowship's bi-monthly magazine *On the 'Beam'* and news of exchanges, parts, events and rallies.

Specification

500cc SUNBEAM S7/S8

ENGINE

Type	ohc in-line twin
Bore x stroke	70 x 63.5mm
Capacity	487cc
Compression ratio	6.5:1 (7.2:1)
Carburation	Amal 15/16in
Bhp @ rpm	25 @ 5800
Primary drive	direct
Clutch	single plate, dry
Gearbox	4 speed
Electrical system	Lucas 60w dynamo, 6v 12a/h battery, coil ignition
Lighting	24/24w headlight

DIMENSIONS

Wheelbase	57in
Seat height	30in
Ground clearance	4.5in (5.5in)
Kerb weight	468lb (inc 1gal fuel)
Fuel capacity	3.5gal
Tyres	
(front)	4.50 x 16 (3.25 x 19) Dunlop
(rear)	4.75 x 15 (4.00 x 18) Dunlop
Brakes	
(front)	8in (7in)
(rear)	8in

PERFORMANCE

Top speed	72mph (78-80mph) approx
Standing ¼ mile	18secs (approx)
Fuel consumption	66mpg
Braking distance	
from 30mph	36ft
from 60mph	136ft
Owner	Tony Wilkins, Leicester

NB: All figures in brackets relate to S8 model, where different.

650cc Triumph Thunderbird

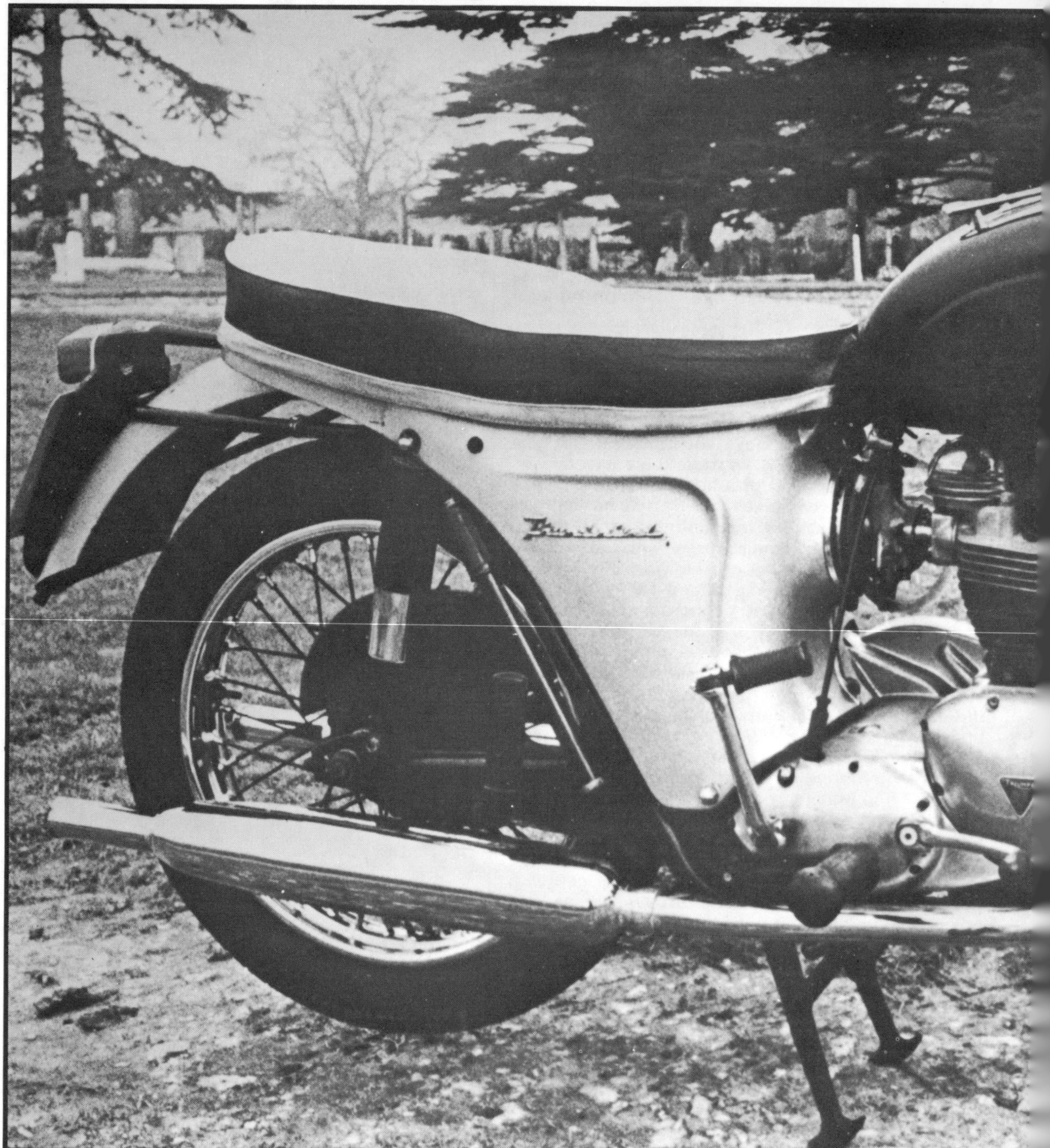

6T by Mike Nicks

Triumph Thunderbird

The point of a motorcycle road test is not to thrash the machine to the verge of destruction, but to use it in a way that a cash-paying customer would, and then attempt to make objective comments about its performance. This might seem a fairly obvious statement, but sometimes it's no wonder that importers and manufacturers grate their teeth when a 100cc trail bike is criticised for not having the power to pull through thick mud, or a V-twin sports machine with hot cams, 40mm carburettors and clip-on handlebars is dismissed as impractical for town use. An intelligent owner isn't going to abuse his purchase in the wrong environment, or flay it so mercilessly that its resale value plummets by a half in 12 months. Neither should a road test subject an engine to 24-hour endurance race treatment.

This prelude explains why the bike which forms the subject of this test was rarely ridden at more than 60 to 65mph, even though it possesses the potential to reach a 100mph speedometer reading without undue hysteria. The 1965 6T Thunderbird was supplied by Porter's Motors of Spalding, Lincs, and has a rather intriguing sort of non-history. The firm supplied it new in August 1965 and bought it back again in May 1967, when the recorded mileage was only 10,600. Porter's knew this to be a genuine figure, as the Thunderbird's only owner had been a local man they saw regularly. Then the bike stood in the shop, unsought after and unsold, through the motorcycle trade's depression years of the late sixties and into the early seventies, when British machinery was regarded as crude trash in the face of Oriental sophistication. Now, when the prices of obsolete British products have been inflated by a combination of pure nostalgia and the realisation that a motorcycle's appeal is based on character as well as advanced technology, Porter's wouldn't sell the Thunderbird anyway! And who could blame them?

Not only does this bike have relatively few miles on its barrels, but its lack of use means that it is in 99.5 per cent original condition. The chrome Thunderbird logo was missing from the left flank of the famous 'bathtub' rear enclosure, and a Continental tyre has been fitted to the rear wheel. Apart from that it was all there, which means that if it was put on the market today it would easily fetch twice its original sale price of £308, and possibly a lot more if the right kind of money-no-object collector happened along.

So there, a collector's item this Thunderbird undoubtedly is, whether or not you agree with the

Probably the most famous British power unit ever, the 650cc parallel twin runs a mild 7:1 compression ratio making it very tractable without losing excitement.

Tank-top luggage carrier was an optional extra at first but soon became standard equipment.

Triumph's attempt to tidy up the handlebar area remains a style that typifies the period.

concept of motorcycles being revered and pampered as such. And that being so, it would only be used as a Sunday morning fun bike, a machine to ride out into the country on a sultry August evening. There are plenty of other oilier, dirtier Triumphs being used as genuine working motorcycles, but the fact remains that it's no longer worth treating this particular bike in that way.

Having become all too aware of this while I examined the 6T with Steve Porter, I settled into the aforementioned 60 to 65mph gait on the road out of Spalding and ruminated briefly on Triumph history. The Thunderbird was the first of the post-war Triumph 650s (there had been the short-lived 649cc Model 6/1 of 1934), having been launched in 1949 with a 34bhp engine and sprung-hub rear end. And as a publicity gesture, three of the new bikes were taken to the Montlhery bowl in France, where they circulated at around 90mph for 500 miles and climaxed the stunt with a final lap at over 100mph.

By 1965 the Thunderbird had inherited unit construction, partial rear-end closure (items which had first appeared in 1957 on the Twenty-One), and a swinging-arm rear end, while Doug Hele had moved to Meriden and drastically improved the suspect handling of the early twins. Also, the Bonneville had taken over the role of Triumph range leader, leaving the faithful Thunderbird as very much the cooking version of the 650s. It remained a single-carb model, and ran a lowly 7.0:1 compression ratio.

In these times when motorcycles with top speeds of over 130mph seem almost commonplace, it's very tempting to wonder why such a mild device as the Thunderbird was able to arouse the affection it did over a prolonged period of years. But remember that the Thunderbird was launched a decade before Britain's first motorway was opened, and even in 1965 when the test bike was manufactured, the motorway network in the UK was still sparse. Most journeys were done on 'A' roads, and if you had a machine that could cruise in the sixties you could set very reasonable average speeds. It was enjoyable stuff, too, matching the speed of your bike to the curves and gradients of a road system that didn't bludgeon its way across the face of the land like modern pre-packaged convenience highways, but curved in harmony with thousands of years of history and geography that had preceded it. There was less importance placed on a vehicle's ability to cruise at continuous high speeds, but it *was* expected to perform in balance with its environment, and in this the Thunderbird clearly succeeded.

In fact it does to this day, providing the convenience routes are ignored. Engine performance is undeniably soft, yet sheer swept volume ensures that the bike has adequate power. Its commendably low weight obviously helps — the 37 horsepower claimed for the 1965 model goes a long way when it has to propel only 375lb of motorcycle. So the Thunderbird can be left in top for most overtaking purposes, pulling away from slow corners, and much urban work. In fact in town it provided cause for reflection on the state of current motorcycle design whenever a trivial item such as a GT250 Suzuki poked ahead to the accompaniment of much two-stroke shrieking and a desperate flashing of brake lights when the next corner appeared. The ageing Thunderbrid, relying on a broad spread of torque and generous engine braking, was able to keep pace and eventually slip ahead when the two-stroke rider inevitably got caught off the power band in the wrong gear at the wrong time. It comes back to that question of balance.

Reacquaintance with a Triumph gearbox was also illuminating. Naturally I forgot the ritual of freeing the clutch on cold. The anguished gnashing when bottom was engaged meant that it was also the last occasion. But even changes between ratios are not without their problems with a Triumph box. Has motorcycling been grossly unfair on BMW over the years, when even the Triumph, the epitome of mainstream British motorcycling, requires a distinct two-stage foot movement if gears are to be engaged silently and sensuously? Any attempt to push through the Triumph change is a notchy sensation that leaves a bad taste of burred riding in the mind. Coax it through, with a milli-second pause halfway through

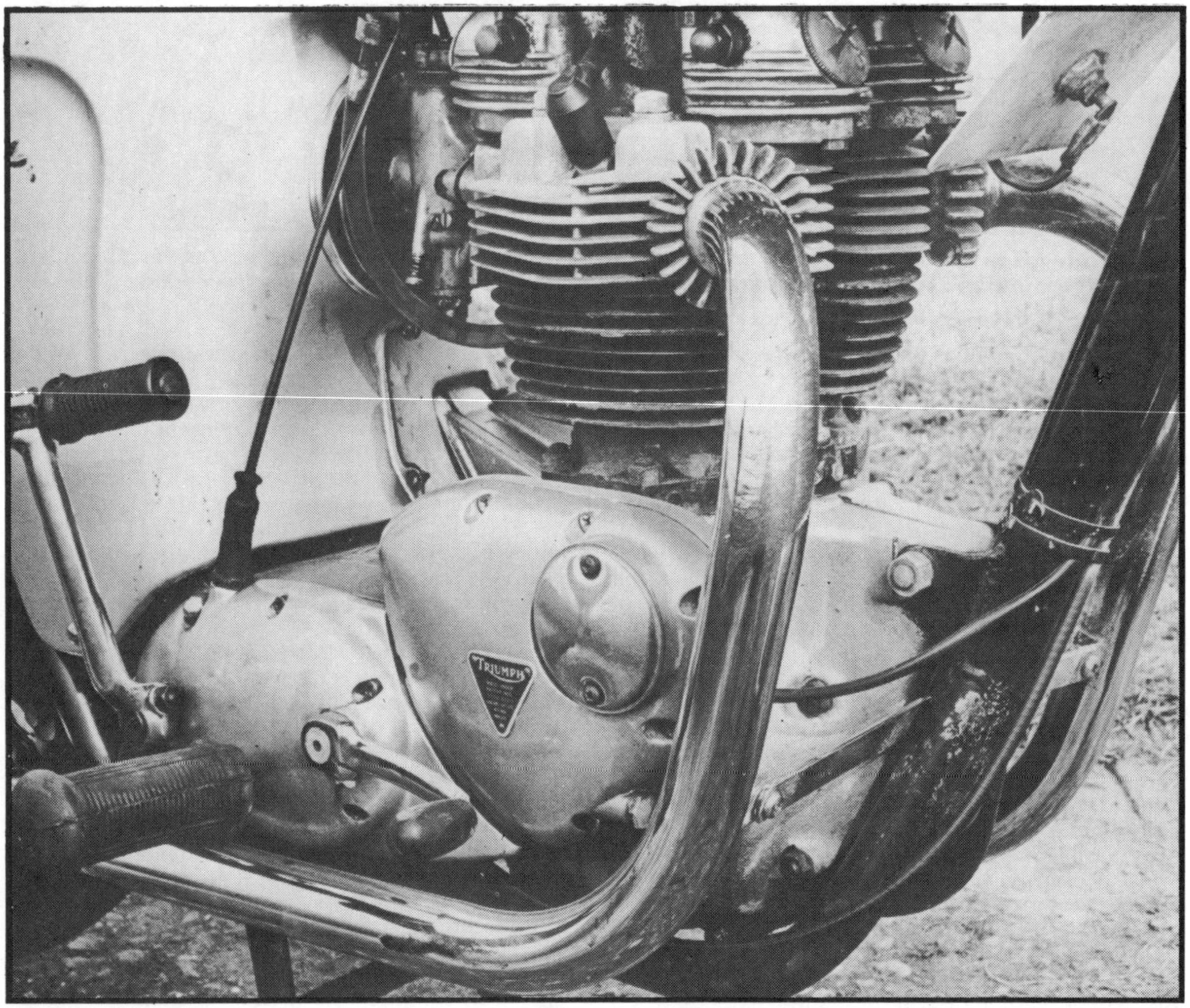

A genuine low mileage motorcycle, this Thunderbird has not been restored, rebuilt or even cleaned up.

Another contribution to the collective motorcycling memory, the most distinctive of all Triumph tank badges.

the movement, and it's a very pleasurable box to use.

Triumph handling had become something of a yardstick by the mid-sixties, with precise, neutral steering, plenty of ground clearance and suspension that was supple enough by the standards of the day. Despite the slender profile of a parallel twin, however, it was always possible to scrub rubber from the footrests and metal from the centre stand without too much effort. Therefore, it was quite a surprise to discover that the underside of the footrest rubbers on this bike — and they were definitely the original fittings — were free of graze marks. The one and only active owner had clearly been a careful man, and even if Steve Porter hadn't forewarned me of the worn rear suspension units it would have seemed sacrilege to violate in a few miles what someone else had left unscathed in 10,000. Serious attempts to lay the bike on to the footrests were consequently forgotten, a decision that was in any case largely preempted by the tired condition of the rear units. They made the ride on rough roads reminiscent of piloting a Harley-Davidson Electra Glide with the sprung saddle, and under power on the exit from corners the back end would lurch like the infamous 'Flexy Flier' two-stroke triple Suzukis in the early days of Formula 750 racing.

Memory recalls that in its time the Thunderbird's bathtub styling gave it a rather ponderous image. Well, nothing is more fickle than the motorcycling public's response to outward appearances, and to me the 6T's lines suggest flowing, clean-cut vigour. The rearward jut of those handlebars that Triumph used for years, the splayed exhaust ports and the aggressive back-sweep of the pipes made the bikes look like they were eager for 80mph even when they were standing still. Viewed from the side, the barrels and rocker covers are surrounded by... space. Think about that; Yamaha designers wanted to give their XS750 transverse triple the same effect when they

A light all-up weight and very useful engine braking means the front brake is adequate for assured and smooth stopping.

The lines seem elegant now though at one time bathtub enclosures were simply ripped off by fashion conscious owners.

were laying it out. They found that the bulkier dohc engine wouldn't allow it, and eventually they filled in the sideways profile of the bike so that it appears as solid metal from the front downtubes back, as do so many Japanese bikes. Yet the 'holes' around the Triumph engine don't look silly, they just add to the Thunderbird's overall graceful theme... take a bow, anonymous Meriden stylist of the time.

Reviews of obsolete motorcycles should not, of course, commit the unforgiveable error of lapsing into drivelling nostalgia. The Thunderbird was and remains a fine motorcycle for medium-speed touring,

By the sixties Doug Hele had worked wonders with the once dubious frame, making the Thunderbird an A-road special.

but leaning too heavily on that 360-degree crankshaft brings retribution. In fact the hallowed Triumph twin tradition of ancillary items dislodging themselves from the motorcycle began within eight miles of the bike being collected. A glance down at the speedometer revealed that the screw attaching the chrome strip to the side of the headlamp nacelle was about to drop into the road. It was retrieved before it was lost, but a half dozen miles later its partner at the other end of the strip worked loose in sympathy. For security's sake I removed the strip for the duration of the test.

More was to come — or come off, should I say. Giving the bike a brief full throttle burst to find out just how a mid-sixties single carb 650 Triumph can perform revealed that the motor would spin freely to 60mph in second gear and 80 in third; absolute test strip speeds in these ratios are probably in the region of 65mph and just over 90mph respectively. The Thunderbird would also batter merrily into the wind at a steady 80mph, but it would not be accurate to say that this was a relaxed speed. In fact at anything over 70mph the engine felt distinctly busy, even though it would pull to an indicated 100 with the rider sitting upright — no mean feat for a pushrod touring bike with an engine specification laid down three decades ago. Well, the Triumph twin was always a quick bike, but the penalty became apparent next morning. On the journey to return the 6T the engine note sounded flat; the air cleaner had unscrewed itself from the carburettor intake, although the bathtub enclosure had stopped it from dropping into the road. In itself the incident was no problem, merely a reminder that real mechanical disasters await Triumph engines that are persistently flogged at the top end of the rev range. The rear pushrod tube also wept a dribble of oil which sat on top of the gearbox casing proclaiming that this was indeed a British motorcycle.

There is no real modern-day equivalent of the Triumph Thunderbird. The middleweight Japanese fours are about speed, in terms of both mph and crankshaft revolutions. The Honda CX500 is perhaps closer to the Thunderbird in the way it performs, but with four-valve cylinder heads, water cooling and shaft drive it hardly ranks as a bottom-of-the-line tourer. And BMWs of any capacity are just too expensive. The Kawasaki Z750 vertical twin isn't even a pleasant motorcycle to ride, with its throttle response severely fuzzed by the effects of balancer shafts and drive-train lash, while Yamaha's XS650 is more of a competitor for the Bonneville. Large capacity, softly-tuned, cheap four-strokes like the Thunderbird are just not built any more, which is a pity because the concept makes for a very nice style of motorcycling. And most people can't handle the power of the flashier stuff properly anyway.

Specification

650cc TRIUMPH THUNDERBIRD 6T

ENGINE

Type	**ohv parallel twin**
Bore x stroke	**71 x 82mm**
Capacity	**649cc**
Compression ratio	**7.0:1**
Carburation	**Amal Monobloc 376**
Bhp @ rpm	**37 @ 6700**
Primary drive	**duplex chain**
Clutch	**multi-plate, wet**
Gearbox	**4 speed**
Electrical system	**12v alternator, battery and coil ignition**

DIMENSIONS

Wheelbase	**55.0in**
Seat height	**30.0in**
Ground clearance	**5.5in**
Kerb weight	**375lb**
Fuel capacity	**4gal**
Tyres	
(front)	**3.25 x 18 Avon SM Mk II**
(rear)	**3.50 x 18 Continental**
Brakes	
(front)	**8in**
(rear)	**7in**

PERFORMANCE

Top speed	**100mph (est)**
Standing ¼ mile	**15.0secs (est)**
Fuel consumption	**61mpg**
Braking distance from 30mph	**31ft**
Owner	**Porter's Motors, Spalding, Lincs.**

500cc Velocette MSS

by Peter Watson

Velocette MSS

It was very still. Through the graveyard darkness I could sense as much as see a dank white mist lapping at the sides of the valley below and the faint glimmer of a reflection off the tarmac surface of the road, twisting down towards the river. An almost imperceptible ticking of metal cooling and contracting shattered the silence. Suddenly a scent of hot Gunk wafted upwards, bringing with it a whole host of memories like a breath of perfume. It was after midnight and I was sitting on a British single at the side of a country road in the very heart of England, just letting time slip pleasantly by. I swung down on the Velo's kickstart, slipped into gear and thudded lazily into the distance.

"The Velocette single," said Royce Creasey, eyeing me steadily, "is the definitive English motorcycle." I remember nodding sagely at the time, while other names and marques drifted across my mind. Friend that Royce is — and contributor to *Classic Bike* — I had to bear in mind that he is possessed of the world's strangest Velocette Venom. But he is, naturally, right. And two weeks with Jim Plant's 1954 499cc MSS convinced me. A Velocette single is just that — the definitive English motorcycle.

Like English politics it evolved slowly and changed almost imperceptibly. Like the English climate it can prove unpredictable, even perverse. Parts of its design display brilliant ingenuity, while other parts are notable for their pigheaded stupidity. A German would have been more logical, an Italian altogether more dashing; only an Englishman could have laid out the Velocette single.

The first Velocette MSS half-litre single was developed from the 348cc MAC model, which in turn was a larger version of the 248cc MOV, Veloce's first single in which overhead valves were operated by pushrods instead of an overhead cam. Quite why this 495cc (81 x 96mm) machine should have been graced with the same SS designation which singled out that all-time classic the 350 KSS, no-one seems to know. It was a 75mph cooking single in an altogether different league.

The Goodmans, who owned Velocette, had wanted to produce a machine that was both cheaper to manufacture than the ohc K series while offering more poke than their sedate 250 GTP two-stroke single. The MOV, launched in 1933, opened up an era of prosperity for a firm that had been putting too much time and effort into producing the best without being able to ask the most for it. Yet the way in which they and their staff operated still raises a laugh.

When the MSS was reintroduced in 1953 — it had previously run from 1935 to 1948 with a break for WW2 — it was in a redesigned, 86 x 86mm form. Alan

High camshaft and short pushrods distinguish the 500cc single, which combines flexibility with punch.

Velocette forks leave something to be desired as far as stiffness is concerned – likewise the brake.

Developed from the rigid KTT frame, the MSS trellis could do with some cross bracing.

Baker, Technical Editor of *Motor Cycle*, naturally assumed, when questioning Velocette development engineer Charles Udall, that the new square dimensions had been born of a significant change of heart.

"Does the 86mm bore and stroke mean that you are now in favour of comparatively short strokes and big bores...?" he enquired hopefully.

"The reason for the changed dimension is very simple," replied Udall gaily. "We decided to use the current MAC spring frame to house the new MSS engine, and the size of this frame is such that the old "long-stroke" engine was too tall to go in — so we shortened its stroke until it would fit."

Baker retreated, doubtless saddened, to a discussion of the crankshaft assembly, pausing to observe that: "I had expected a technical lecture and had received a straightforward admission of expediency!"

Pragmatic engineering is hardly an exclusively English vice, but we were its leading exponents at one time. Witness the primary and final drive layout of the MSS. With a single-row, caged-roller big end and tapered roller mains and a primary driveline as close to the centreline of the engine as possible — inside the final drive which begins with a sprocket outboard of the clutch — the Velo single has an immensely strong, stiff bottom end. It's also child's play to change a sprocket and the overall gear ratio.

Yet this narrow chain-line, for so long a Velocette trademark, had its disadvantages in that it seriously restricted space for the clutch. Enter therefore, stage left, the infamous Hall Green clutch. As the service manual puts it: "Before attempting any adjustment of the clutch it is important that the operation of the clutch is fully understood..." But of course. When you have to take off a pressed steel cover to reveal the gearbox sprocket and then thrust a special steel peg through one of three holes about its centre, locate that in one of the spring carrier's castellations behind and then move the rear wheel backwards or forwards, depending upon whether the clutch is slipping or dragging, it calls for some thought. And if that fails to produce a satisfactory result you must consult one of the other three pages that deal with the adjusting procedure in a mildly hectoring tone. It's weird; it also slips when subjected to the full force of a Thruxton's 41bhp, and if you hold it out in traffic for extended periods the tiny thrust bearing gives up the ghost.

And yet... the Velocette clutch is light and operates sweetly enough if you don't abuse it, acting as a perfect complement to the long-throw, four speed box. This is a one-up, three-down device of great antiquity and charm whose internals can still be encountered on the Silk two-stroke. Its delicate feel but firmly positive engagement are inimitable.

And that engine. It climbs up under the black tank with its gold lining and disappears from view. All you can see are the massive fins of the barrel, the short pushrod tower and the Y constructed by it and the short external oil lines. It's a tall, very quiet unit with carefully meshed and very long-lasting helical timing gears transferring the crankshaft motion to a camshaft set high in the crankcase, with short, substantial pushrods. Valve springs are KTT racer-style hairpins. Instead of a chain, the drive to the forward-mounted dynamo is via a flat belt, with the driving pulley forming part of the engine shaft shock absorber assembly, a spring-loaded face-cam arrangement.

Naturally Jim Plant, 33-year-old secretary of the Velocette Owners' Club spares scheme, has made plenty of changes to his 1954 MSS. They're the sort of changes that any thinking Velo owner makes, subtle yet effective.

Instead of an automatic advance/retard Lucas K1F magneto drive off that fibre gear which always seems to strip its teeth at the most inconvenient of times, he has substituted a BTH manual control mag with steel driving gear. The dynamo drive belt is the later, vee type which slips less readily than the flat one, but they still break occasionally. I've ridden an experimental factory-built Venom with alternator and toothed-belt drive. Replacing the 36-watt Miller DVR 6-volt dynamo with its automatic voltage control on its back is a 40-watt Lucas item disguised as a Miller unit and feeding a JG electronic voltage step-up conversion mounted on the toolbox. This provides 12-volt lighting and a remarkably loud noise from the 6-volt Lucas Altette horn. Cunningly concealed inside the hollowed-out hard rubber case of an original Exide 6-volt battery is a smaller modern Japanese 12-volt unit.

Other mods include wide-ratio gears — it should be the pre-war close ratio cluster as used later on the Venom — a screwed-up primary chaincase, breathers from oil tank and crankcase as fitted to machines after 1967, and a Monobloc instead of the separate float chamber 276 Amal carburettor. The chain case still leaks oil, while the rest of the motor remained clean and tight, but the Monobloc is a definite improvement on the weeping 276.

Jim Plant knows the history of his MSS, one of nine Velocettes he owns. With an engine number that reads MSS 10359 he knows that it was the 359th to roll out of the Birmingham factory in 1954. Production of the MSS ceased in 1971 when all Velocette manufacture came to an end. It was delivered to the Dene Motor Co in Newcastle-on-Tyne and registered on April 7. What happened to it between then and the day that Jim Plant bought it for just £1.50 in 1973, is anyone's guess, but it was a yellow-painted wreck

Though manufactured in 1954 the MSS exudes a distinctly vintage air when seen from this angle.

The definitive English motorcycle? Debate may rage but the Velocette MSS typifies a now departed epoch.

Velocette MSS

resting in someone's garden. He rebuilt it to this immaculate standard and since he's owned it the engine has been down at least three times. It felt just right: crisp and gentle, willing to plod along in top at little more than walking pace or wind up to just under 82mph on the test track, precisely the figure *Motor Cycling*'s test model achieved in 1954.

With its heavy flywheels, mild cam — providing a mere 38 degrees overlap — and 6.8:1 piston, the MSS is quick off the line and deliciously flexible right up to the point where it simply runs out of breath. A comfortable cruising speed turned out to be an indicated 60 or a true 56mph, at which speed a sound as mellow as 12-year-old scotch and as solid as rump steak issues from the fish-tail silencer. The stepped dual seat, derived so closely from the pre-war sprung saddle and pillion pad in shape, is delightfully comfortable. With slightly forward mounted footrests and flattish, pulled-back bars, I felt really secure and passengers commented very favourably on the legroom provided by their perch. Later dual seats are much harder.

Naturally the MSS featured Phil Irving's clever idea for varying the spring preload on the Woodhead-Monroe shock absorbers, where the upper location can be moved through an arc of adjustment. Fully forward naturally provides the lightest pre-load and a position roughly central can cope with two medium-sized people. Ground clearance, like the lock, is fairly restricted and once or twice I felt the centre-stand touch down on bumpy curves.

In fact the frame, examined in detail, shows something of a lack of stiffness at the rear to say the very least. When the post-war spring frame was designed for the 348cc MAC, Velocette selected a rigid cradle based around KTT practice and merely welded a tubular lug to the back of the saddle tube through which passed a spindle bearing on two plain phosphor bronze bushes. These are frequently short-lived. Attached to either end of the spindle by a split-clamp arrangement are the two separate tubular arms that make up the swinging fork. Above them lies greater weakness in the form of no real cross-bracing of the rear subframe. There is, it's true, a tubular steel tie with flattened ends, but the fact that the chromed steel mudguard stays have a habit of fracturing tells its own tale about what's going on at the back end under hard cornering on poor surfaces. Velocette's

Inboard clutch and pressed tin covers were both annoying – one to adjust, the other to seal effectively.

mod for long-distance events like the 100mph-plus 24-hour Venom stunt was a stronger tie-piece.

Not that you really feel any of these deficiencies on the MSS. It's beautifully smooth up to 55mph when vibration gets steadily worse, pounding in through the bars and footrests. Yet a Velo shakes more than vibrates in that nasty parallel twin fashion. Nothing came loose or fell off, unlike a Venom I once rode which attempted to deposit its carburettor on the road.

Perhaps the worst aspects of the bike, which was in superb condition, were the brakes and front forks. And I'd naturally be mentioning the lights but for that 12-volt conversion and Lucas car-type headlight. The braking area of Mr Plant's MSS is 21.5sq in, while the later Viper 350 single featuring full-width drums has 33.75sq in. In urban conditions I took Jim Plant's advice and stayed well clear of other traffic. The need to stop suddenly was, on occasion, met with what you might call an on-going situation. Those Velocette forks, introduced in 1951 after the Dowty Oleomatics had been dropped, may offer an offset axle and reasonable movement, but they felt spindly and poorly damped. Looking down while running flat out through our timing lights, I was greeted with the not altogether welcome sight of the fork legs whipping backwards and forwards in a truly alarming manner. The front wheel may have needed balancing: I don't think Jim Plant regularly puts down 82mph on the road...

There's definitely something that, well, *gets to you* about Velocettes, if you know what I mean. In the past Norton singles, which are in some respects big, brutal, masculine versions of the ideal that Velocette represent, have been my favourites. But Velos have a very different character, epitomised by the ritualistic starting procedure and the long, swinging kick necessitated by a kickstart that is ridiculously low-geared. And the MSS — and certainly this particular example — represents that happy medium between going so slowly that you fall asleep and going so fast that things fall off in the rush. I'd love to own it, but Jim Plant definitely isn't selling...

If you own a Velocette already then you should naturally be a member of the owners club. Membership secretary is Ted Snelling at 3 Handley Road, Mitcham, Surrey. For your money you'll get their excellent *Fishtail* magazine and membership of the spares scheme as well as all the help and support that only a good one-make club can provide. The club's spares manufacturing and supply company, Veloce Spares Ltd, is expanding all the time.

I run down the road across the valley pretty regularly these days. It's part of one of my favourite roads. But whenever I pass the spot where I stopped to let the feel of the definitive English motorcycle sink into my mind, I remember that night. And how pleasant it felt just to be alive.

Specification

1954 VELOCETTE MSS

ENGINE

Type	ohv single
Bore x stroke	86 x 86mm
Capacity	499cc
Compression ratio	6.8:1
Carburation	$1\frac{1}{16}$in Amal Monobloc
Bhp @ rpm	23 @ 5000
Primary drive	Single row chain
Clutch	Multi-plate, wet
Gearbox	4 speed
Electrical system	BTH manual advance/retard magneto. Lucas 40w dynamo with JG 12v conversion.
Lighting	45/50w headlight

DIMENSIONS

Wheelbase	54.5in
Seat height	31in
Overall width	30in
Ground clearance	5.25in
Kerb weight	390lb (inc 1gal fuel)
Fuel capacity	3gal
Tyres	
(front)	3.25 x 19 Dunlop K70
(rear)	3.25 x 19 Dunlop K70
Brakes	
(front)	7in sls drum
(rear)	7in sls drum

PERFORMANCE

Top speed prone	81.74mph
Standing $\frac{1}{4}$ mile	18.46 sec
Speedometer error	
at indicated 30mph	29.15mph
at indicated 60mph	55.97mph
Fuel consumption	
overall	58mpg
ridden hard	50mpg
Braking distance	
from 30mph	35ft
from 60mph	158ft
Owner	Jim Plant, Birmingham.

1000cc Vincent Rapide and 500cc Comet

by Royce Creasey

Vincent Rapide and Comet

The Vincent V-twin is unquestionably the high point of the English motorcycle industry. Its reappearance in the late forties should have resulted in the immediate demise of the parallel twin and shown up the revered Norton Featherbed frame for the 'damn great trellis' that it is. That neither of these things happened is a further indictment of both the industry and the people who bought its products.

Both Vincent and the original HRD company were progressive; the Rapide had hydraulically damped suspension at both ends before most of the competition even had suspension at both ends. HRD were fitting the now common cantilever type rear suspension by 1928, although public objection to rear springing was the main reason for this choice of layout — it could be made to look like a rigid! Possibly more important was the fact that the creators of the machine were both riders as well as designers and manufacturers, a rare event in post-war corporations. Even the inevitable accountant seems to have been enthusiastic about the product.

The 1,000cc model tested is a 1947 Series B Rapide, updated to 1949 C specification principally by the addition of Girdraulic front forks and a rear damper. The Rapide could be considered as the equivalent of the T3 in the Guzzi range, or perhaps the Darmah of the Ducati stable. Although derived from the pre-war A series, the B is the result of a most thorough redesign and a degree of cost-no-object elaboration which is unlikely ever to be equalled in the realms of motorcycle manufacturing. This work was carried out with the single intention of making an already good machine work better for longer, and when introduced in 1946 the Rapide was the fastest production machine in the world. Well documented tests have seen 100,000 miles pass without major parts in the engine having to be replaced.

There is nothing like enough room in this test to permit consideration of this bike in full detail, but some idea of the degree of refinement that went into it can be gained by examining one of the simpler components — the rear wheel. Although not qd in the accepted sense, it can be removed in minutes using only a pair of pliers for the chain link. Torque arms for the twin brakes are retained by spring clips, and slackening the tommy bar on the axle allows the chain adjusters to be taken up by hand. Each click of the adjusters provides for about 300 miles of use. The wheel will fit either way round, has two sprockets to give alternative ratios and runs on adjustable rollers.

This kind of detailed thinking pervades the whole bike, and the adjustability extends to assembly set-

Nuts, bolts, cables, levers and brace-bars give the drive side of the Rapide a very busy appearance.

The famous Vincent speedometer which might just be useful over its whole range.

Girdraulic front forks were an attempt to combine the rigidity of girders with the comfort of telescopics.

tings. Half-time pinions come in .001in steps, over- and under-size, to get that timing gear backlash just right. Elaboration at this level can be criticised as extremely expensive, resulting in high prices, low sales — and eventual extinction. It is probable that if more thought had been devoted to the production engineering side of the Vincent, costs could have been reduced without cheapening the bike, yet the Rapide justifies itself simply by still being here, thirty years later.

Apart from this detailing, which current fashion increasingly decries and is only of interest when the bike is not being ridden there is the matter of the basic design. Messrs Vincent and Irving were more than progressive; they also had theories, and the chief among them was that wheel spindles should always stay in line. The necessary stiffness to achieve this was the chief target of the post-war rethink. Frame flexing was dealt with at source by the removal of the frame; the headstock is fixed to a sheet-metal triangular oil tank which bolts to the cylinder heads and picks up the rear suspension struts. Words like 'neat' help one avoid becoming emotional when considering the elegance of this solution. The front forks are a similarly clever attempt to combine the rigidity of girders with the ride of telescopics, and include forged high-duty alloy blades. Modern thought indicates that keeping the wheels on the ground may be more useful than the benefits offered by the Vincent arrangement, and the Girdraulics on the Rapide are stuck with a high unsprung weight when compared with contemporary telescopic forks. In practice, the immense stiffness and stability of the Vincent design easily compensates for the slightly poorer ride, and the complete absence of dive under braking is an advantage that telescopics cannot match.

The suspension quality of the Girdraulics unfortunately relies on careful maintenance, although bearing life is around 20,000 miles, similar to that on the latest telescopics. It is very probable that the reputation the Vincent gained in the sixties for developing killer wobbles at speed was the result of unmaintained forks in what the VOC would probably call 'the wrong hands'. Anomalies in the design include mounting the headlight and speedo unsprung, and fitting cup 'n' cone head bearings when taper rollers appear everywhere else. Purpose-built Koni dampers are available for the Girdraulics, and indeed all the Vincent suspensions, and the level of performance is such that it would not be absurd for Ducati (for instance) to seriously consider an updated version of this fork for next year's model.

The rear suspension doesn't quite reach the standard of the front end, probably because when the cantilever layout was introduced it was so much better than anything else that no one noticed it wasn't perfect. Wheel control is fine, it's just a little flexible, and consideration of the rear fork reveals uncharacteristic

Vincent Rapide and Comet

lapses such as curved tubes and an absence of bracing. Carrying a passenger increases the flex considerably, as the rear seat supports act as levers on the fork, a defect that was cured on the later D model when the seat was mounted on a more conventional subframe. None of the passengers carried seemed to notice the unsprung nature of their end of the seat — numbed minds were more common than numbed backsides as a reaction to the Vincent experience.

The engine is undoubtedly the main visual attraction on the big Vincents. Its design is less than perfect; what can reasonably be described as over-elaboration causes its own problems in terms of fragility in some parts and very high rebuild costs. Technology has passed by the hemispherical head, and in theory the Vincent's output and fuel and oil consumption do not meet modern standards. In practice it is a very pleasant device indeed, having the best match of bike, flywheel and reciprocating weights I've yet encountered. Flexibility and response are exceptional, the transmission is snatch-free, and the degree of engine braking is just right. The rider can vary the output from just enough to keep the flywheels topped up whilst floating round town, to what has been justifiably described as 'constant and colossal' from nowhere to much too fast. The test Rapide is run regularly and was consequently in good adjustment. Starting in the morning was normally a one-kick affair and although its owner, Jack Barker (the social secretary of the VOC), told me it leaked oil, I never did find out where.

The gearchange suffers from the possibility of play between the positive stop and the selector cam, while a dragging clutch can make first impossible to engage even though the lever moves. At speed the change is delicate and a little slow, kidding you that it's better than it is until you relax and it rejects your selection. The clutch drag on Jack's machine was caused by new shoes, which improved considerably during the 600 miles of the test as they bedded in.

Shoes..? On a clutch..? Yes, well the Vincent clutch takes off where Hall Green gave up, and what's more it was all done on purpose. Deciding that 45bhp and a lot of torque were too much for the hand-operated clutches of the day, the design team settled on an all-power mechanical servo device as the solution. This component uses engine power to hold the friction surfaces together, while the lever connects and disconnects engine power. In extremely crude terms it works thus: engine power is fed into a simple single-plate clutch, and the output from this clutch can be considered as turning the actuating cam of a conventional drum brake. The 'brake shoes' are connected to the gearbox and the 'brake drum' to the engine. Simple, innit? Keen students will immediately spot that it can't be that easy and may rest assured that it isn't. In practice the primary clutch, which loads torque into the main clutch, will drive the bike up to around 50mph, and centrifugal force assists marginally at the highest engine speeds. It's really worth reading up on the subject just to see how far out of hand clutch design can get. Servo clutches traditionally suffer from various ills — they include sensitivity to weather conditions and a fairly random mode of operation. All these defects are detectable in the Vincent unit, but in entirely bearable moderation. The rest of the world would appear to have been better advised in either improving friction materials until they could take large power outputs or, more rarely, providing for servo actuation of a heavily sprung conventional clutch. This is the Velocette method, although it may have been an accident.

In engineering terms the Vincent clutch is unsupportable, but in practice it justifies its presence by providing a whole lot of fun. The Cosmic Supply Company must have had a hand in its origination, as the first touch of the primary clutch plates guarantees that anything may take place, from gradual, automatic take-up to 100 per cent connection between two firing pulses. An incidental advantage of all this uncertainty is that the evident concentration of the rider as a Vincent moves off the line acts as a complete deterrent to would-be racers. They invariably mistake the Vincent man's attempt to be gentle with expensive and ageing machinery for fear that wheelspin and wheelie will occur simultaneously! Incidentally, the engine, transmission and frame all seem to be quite capable of standing up to the vagaries of the clutch's performance.

Once the Vincent is rolling, however, these considerations of various oily bits of machinery become progressively irrelevant. With the bike at a standstill, the motor sounds like a worn-out tractor as it ticks over, as do Porsche and Coventry-Climax engines. But by the time the mid-eighties have been reached, all the rider is conscious of is a distant thunder, and the universe rippling past. Even moderate use of more throttle at this speed gives the impression that the bike is still while the horizon is being dragged helplessly closer. The noise levels produced by a stately but determined lift-off are of the sort commonly associated with the appearance of cracks in the road and collapsing buildings — Godzilla speaks when a Vincent moves! The heavy flywheels allow short bursts of throttle to carry the bike a considerable distance in almost complete silence, and the rider frequently arrives in the situation of overtaking other vehicles while the engine is on the over-run.

In terms of the riding experience, it is true of most of the English classics that they accomplish little that is not done better by other machines, but generally

The 500cc Comet carries the same running gear as its bigger brother and the performance suffers for it.

A legend in its lifetime and a myth afterwards, the Rapide seems to be speeding effortlessly even at rest.

Vincent Rapide and Comet

excel at managing everything rather well. This thirty-year-old Rapide does almost everything as well as the best moderns, and some things better. Fitted with Avon Roadrunners and longer than standard Petteford springs to improve ride and ground clearance, the stability at extreme angles of lean is exceptional. Both ends begin to drift simultaneously, the high degree of stiffness permits easy control, and the bike leaves corners exactly on line. If a wrong line is chosen, correction can be carried out without the bike lapsing into weave or plunge, although the front forks can be confused by sudden movements. In particular, tight corners get the bike a little out of shape if taken by storm; the 'slow in, fast out' approach pays off, as the big Vincent needs to be poured rather than thrown into turns.

This excellent controlability and the engine's massive torque are matched by the plunge-free performance of the braking system which, although badly affected by water, is the match of the best double-disc units I've tried. It's true that these drums would fade first on the race track, but on the road the ease with which the front tyre can be just squealed right up to the point of slipping into a corner is virtually unique. At speed the steering needs pushing into turns, and although the Vincent front end is often accused of being heavy at low speed, the feel from the front tyre is very good. Tight corners in urban back streets require an application of the rear brakes to lighten the steering, but the lever pressure is high and more sensitivity would be useful. I am an enthusiastic supporter of this sort of handling, and the similarity of feel between the Velocette Venom and the Rapide is uncanny. In curves the two bikes follow exactly similar lines, the Vincent drifting a little further out due to its slightly higher weight — which is far lower than any current production one-litre motorcycle.

In the period that the Vincent was being made the best roads in the country were of the type now considered lesser A roads. They were two-lane black-tops, with hills and curves and little villages. The A4155 from Sonning to Henley in Berkshire is an example, and running down it on the Rapide one evening at speeds I'm definitely not going to discuss qualifies as one of the year's great trips. The bike followed the road so easily that I had little to do but sit there, moving fingers and toes, mind blowing in the breeze. On more modern roads speeds are limited as usual by rider fatigue, and constant fast riding on these routes would require some sort of fairing such as the interesting bodywork fitted to the later D series Black Prince. There are certainly several bikes that can attain a higher speed sooner than the Rapide, but very few that could match it cross-country over long distances.

The little relative of the V-twins, the 500cc Comet, uses identical cycle parts. The minor difference in wheelbase is the result of detail alterations to the crankcase mountings, a cast bridge replacing the rear cylinder as a structural member. More importantly, the flywheels are essentially similar to those fitted to the larger engines, and this huge excess of weight overwhelms the single's output. The result feels like an Edwardian BSA B40, and the Comet is an example of how easy it is to spoil a good package by changing a part of it. Naturally, the brakes and handling are very good, while the lower weight makes the Comet appreciably faster round tight corners than the Rapide. But the overall effect of the bike is still spoiled by its meagre power delivery. Until fairly high engine revs are reached throttle movement merely results in more noise being generated as the engine attempts to speed up the flywheels, and although the bike seems quite fast it lacks the balance of the better 500s from other manufacturers. The lack of that so-interesting servo clutch reduces the fun still further, and I have to say that I found the Comet a considerable disappointment.

It is traditional to provide some kind of summary of a bike under test, perhaps rating it against its contemporaries. But during the Vincent's period of manufacture there were no comparable machines, it was that far ahead of anything else being made. Turning to the designs produced in any period, we discover a few motorcycles that work so well that the rider can forget that a machine is involved. This is the end to which the best bikes have always aimed, the supply of an unequalled sensation with the minimum of interference from horrid machinery. These bikes can be counted on the fingers and come almost exclusively from Europe. They are regarded with what amounts to reverence by the riders who have experienced them, and are typically produced in rather smaller numbers than the 'superbikes' that flood the market. They are the few. The Vincent V-twin was the first of the few.

A solution looking for problems or a far sighted piece of design? Whatever, the big vee-twin motor looks beautiful.

With no rear cylinder to pick up the backbone, the Comet relies on a cast bridging piece to tie the ends together.

Specification

1947 VINCENT RAPIDE
(modified to 1949 spec)

ENGINE

Type	50 deg high cam V-twin
Bore x stroke	84 x 90mm
Capacity	998cc
Compression ratio	7.5:1
Carburation	2 x $1\frac{1}{8}$in Amal Monobloc
Bhp @ rpm	45 @ 5,300
Ignition	Lucas KVF GM1 magneto
Primary drive	Triplex chain
Clutch	self-servo, single-plate
Gearbox	4 speed

DIMENSIONS

Frame	engine used as main frame member
Suspension	Girdraulic front forks; cantilever rear end
Tyres	
(front)	3.60 x 19 Avon Roadrunner
(rear)	4.10 x 19 Avon Roadrunner
Brakes	
(front)	2 x 7in sls drums
(rear)	2 x 7in sls drums
Wheelbase	56.5in
Seat height	33in
Gound clearance	6in
Dry weight	468lb
Fuel capacity	$3\frac{1}{2}$gal

PERFORMANCE

Top speed	110mph (est)
Standing $\frac{1}{4}$ mile	14.0secs (est)
Fuel consumption	48mpg
Owner	Jack Barker, Gloucestershire.

1950 VINCENT COMET

ENGINE

Type	high cam single
Bore x stroke	84 x 90mm
Capacity	499cc
Compression ratio	6.8:1
Carburation	$1\frac{1}{8}$in Amal Monobloc
Bhp @ rpm	28 @ 5,800
Ignition	Lucas K1F magneto
Primary drive	single-row chain
Clutch	multi-plate
Gearbox	4 speed

DIMENSIONS

Frame	engine used as main frame member
Suspension	Girdraulic front forks, cantilever rear end
Tyres	
(front)	3.60 x 19 Avon Roadrunner
(rear)	4.10 x 19 Avon Roadrunner
Brakes	
(front)	2 x 7in sls drums
(rear)	2 x 7in sls drums
Wheelbase	55.75in
Seat height	33in
Ground clearance	6in
Dry weight	390lb
Fuel capacity	$3\frac{1}{2}$gal

PERFORMANCE

Top speed	90mph (est)
Standing $\frac{1}{4}$ mile	18.0secs (est)
Fuel consumption	70mpg